Praise for
Spirit Circle Games:
A guidebook for mediumship development circles

"A rare guide into developing and creating mediumship circles, while strengthening your own psychic gifts. Spelled out in easy-to-read instructions and simple but effective exercises this is a must read for anyone wishing to begin or further their abilities with others!"

— Melanie Barnum, psychic, medium and author of *The Book of Psychic Symbols*, *Psychic Abilities for Beginners*, *The Steady Way to Greatness* and the Psychic Symbol Oracle Cards

"Whether you're seeking your own development, or looking for a resource as a teacher, *Spirit Circle Games* is a staple for your bookshelf. This guidebook thoroughly hits all aspects of conducting a development circle, all-the-while making the process fun, rich, and rewarding! I wish I had this book when I was operating my own circle!"

— Travis Sanders, clairvoyant, teacher and author of *I Am Psychic, So Are You!* and *Practical Mediumship*

"A delightful read full of practical, yet creative and fun, exercises for the development of mediumship and psychic abilities. The guidelines for facilitating a spirit circle are both helpful and important for maintaining group trust and connection with Spirit.

Bartlett provides numerous exercises that are detailed and straightforward, making this a great resource for anyone who wishes to lead a circle, build their own mediumistic skills or teach these skills to others.

A wise and approachable book, covering an extensive array of approaches designed to enhance and strengthen Spirit communication."

— Jeannette Hill, medium and intuitive guide

"Rev. Bartlett caught my attention with this book. Not only do they spell out the nature of so many types of intuition and psychic skills here, they make it a fun pursuit in a group setting.

This is the perfect time for a book like this when so many people are seeking to connect to their spiritual side and to the Great Consciousness that unites us all. What they have done is translate formally esoteric and mysterious skillsets into a practical guide that shows the way for anyone to learn them. Nicely done."

— Octavia Brooks, shamanic success mentor

"A marvelous job of covering the basics of mediumship development circles, while providing great instruction to take Spiritualist mediumship to the next level. Valuable techniques and exercises for both beginners and leaders to grow their mediumship through this time-honored way: the home circle."

— Susan Fiandach and Connie Wake, authors of *Everyday Conversations: They Key to the Contemporary Medium* books and psychic medium teachers

Spirit Circle Games:

A guidebook for mediumship development circles

Other books by the author

Intuitive Symbols Coloring Book: Unlock your intuition through meditative coloring

The Spiritual Symbols Workbook: Create your personal dictionary of intuitive, psychic and metaphysical symbols

Led by Light: How to develop your intuitive mediumship abilities, Book One

Led by Light: A medium's guide to developing your intuitive and psychic senses, Book Two

Spirit Energy: Table tipping, trumpet voices, trance channeling and other phenomena of physical mediumship

Signs from Spirit Journal: Communicate with your intuition, guides and loved ones in Spirit through signs and symbols in your everyday life

Spirit Circle Games:

A guidebook for mediumship development circles

Rev. Joanna Bartlett

Copyright © 2019 Joanna Bartlett

All Rights Reserved. This book or any portion thereof may not be reproduced or used in any manner whatsoever without the express written permission of the publisher.

Cover image by Image by Tomislav Jakupec from Pixabay

Publisher's Cataloging-in-Publication Data

Names: Bartlett, Joanna, author.

Title: Spirit circle games : a guidebook for mediumship development circles / Rev. Joanna Bartlett.

Description: Eugene, OR : Alight Press, 2019.

Identifiers: LCCN 2019908429 | ISBN 978-1-945489-14-3 (paperback) | ISBN 978-1-945489-15-0 (ebook)

Subjects: LCSH: Mediums. | Extrasensory perception. | Psychic ability. | Spiritualism. | Occultism. | Supernatural. | BISAC: BODY, MIND & SPIRIT / Channeling & Mediumship. | BODY, MIND & SPIRIT / Parapsychology / ESP (Clairvoyance, Precognition, Telepathy). | BODY, MIND & SPIRIT / Spiritualism. | BODY, MIND & SPIRIT / Supernatural.

Classification: LCC BF1286 .B37 2019 (print) | LCC BF1286 (ebook) | DDC 133.9/1--dc23.

Alight Press LLC
Eugene, OR 97405
www.alightpress.com

Printed in the United States of America

Contents

Introduction 1
Benefits of a development circle 4
Starting a development circle 6
    Types of development circles 7
    What abilities you want to develop 12
    Circle logistics 13
    Setting guidelines and expectations 19
    Finding circle participants 25
    Circle checklist 29
    Circle Guidelines example document 30
Running a circle 36
    Roles 37
    Format 39
Connecting with Spirit 44
    Opening and closing the circle 45
    Setting your intention and boundaries 47
    Connecting with your divine self 48
Mediumship development circle exercises 52
    Beginning the exercises 53
    Ending the exercises 54
General mediumship development exercises 56
    Billet readings 58

Index card readings 61
Hot potato readings 64
The power of 3 66
Claircognizance developing exercises 68
Inspired writing 70
Define your symbols 74
Clairvoyance developing exercises 79
Send and receive images 81
Use photographs 85
Sense each other's color 88
Read auras 90
Strengthen and focus your third eye 94
Clairaudience developing exercises 96
Follow the instrument 98
Listen to the sounds around you 100
Imagine sounds 103
Tune into Spirit FM 107
Clairgustance developing exercises 110
Develop your intuitive sense of taste 112
Imagine tastes 115
Ask for tastes from Spirit 118
Clairalience developing exercises 120
Smell each other's energy 122
Imagine smells 124
Strengthen your sense of smell 127

- Ask for smells from Spirit 130
- Clairsentience developing exercises 132
  - Send and receive emotions 134
  - Sense the presence of others 139
  - Go inward into your body 143
  - Extend your awareness 147
  - Get information through your energy centers 151
  - Psychometry: sense the energy of objects 155
  - Medical intuition 159
  - Play intuitive Q&A 162
- Physical mediumship 165
  - How physical mediumship works 166
  - Table tipping 170
  - Dowsing 177
  - Spoon bending 186
- Conclusion 191
- References and further reading 193
- Thanks and acknowledgements 194
- About the author 196
- Stay in touch 197

Introduction

If you're reading this book, you hopefully know what a mediumship development circle is and what it does.

Mediumship is the connection to and communication with those on the other side of life—people who've died in their physical form and are now in Spirit. Mediumship allows us to connect with their energy and communicate information and share emotions (mostly love).

A mediumship development circle is the best way to unfold and develop your mediumship abilities. The definition is really in its name: a gathering of a like-minded and like-hearted group of people who want to work on developing their mediumship. It's called a circle because you usually sit in a circle.

A development circle isn't the only way to advance your mediumship abilities, of course.

Classes—whether online or in person—are wonderful. They allow your teacher to share direct knowledge and information about mediumship. Books are great, too. As an author of several books about mediumship and intuition development, I'm quite partial to books.

Additionally, time spent in meditation, connecting with your inner self and Spirit guides is always time well spent and can be instructive in and of itself.

However, none of these things, alone or even in combination, is really enough to propel your mediumship development to the level it needs to be in order to receive clear

Introduction

communication from those in Spirit. A development circle is the crucial piece needed to make that happen.

In fact, all these things—classes, books, regular mediation and a development circle—are the necessary ingredients in the development of mediumship.

There aren't any shortcuts.

Developing your mediumship skills takes time. It takes effort. You have to make the space in your life for it. You also must be willing to make the changes that will naturally come about as a result of allowing yourself to develop this gift.

Changes? Yes. Changes. Imagine you have the gift of a wonderful singing voice that you decide to develop. As you learn about your voice, how it works and what it needs to be healthy, there will be some behaviors you release and no longer engage in: screaming loudly at sports games, perhaps, or smoking cigarettes. You learn to protect your instrument and treat it with respect, so that it can perform for you at its best. The same goes for your mediumship abilities. As you develop them, you'll learn there are behaviors and choices that will hamper your gift—from foods you eat, to distractions you use to avoid dealing with the pains of life, to the people you allow to be around you.

Change is often terrifying for most of us. But know that if you're asking the universe for your highest good, that's what you'll get. So, any changes are ultimately in your favor and are helping you grow and develop on your spiritual path in this life.

One of the many benefits of sitting in a development circle is that you build a community, so you'll have like-hearted, kindred spirits with whom to move through the changes in your life. I've seen it happen time and again in the circles I've sat in. I've done my fair share of going through change myself: jobs,

Introduction

cities, even marriages. And I've witnessed and supported plenty of my fellow developing mediums experience change, too.

So, let's get on with learning about mediumship development circles. This book will show you the benefits of sitting in a development circle, give you some options and guidelines on setting up your own circle—including how to find people, setting participant's expectations and boundaries, and how to run the thing—and then go into a series of exercises that will keep things fun and interesting when your development circle meets. I'll cover some general mediumship development exercises, as well as ones that focus on each of the intuitive or psychic senses: clairvoyance, clairsentience, claircognizance, clairaudience, clairalience and clairgustance.

Some of the content of this book comes from other books of mine, including the *Led by Light* intuitive mediumship development series and *Spirit Energy*. Other exercises are compiled from ones I've used in circles I've taught or sat in, or from talking with other professional mediums.

As with all my books and classes, I'll close this introduction with this: I'll share what I know to be the truth for me. Take from it what works for you. I trust you to know your own truth. That's half the point of developing your abilities to begin with: to be able to listen to your own internal sense of rightness and learn to follow it.

Benefits of a development circle

A mediumship development circle has many benefits, some that are quite unexpected. While one of the expected benefits is developing your gifts, a necessary byproduct is the ability to get into a meditative state much easier than before, due to the sheer amount of practice you'll have at doing it. This, then allows you to experience life in a different way. Meditation helps you become calmer and more able to appreciate life—as does connecting with people in Spirit who share their wisdom and much wider perspective on life and death than we're often able to appreciate in our biodegradable soul sacs.

Meditating with others has even more benefit than meditating alone, in that you're able to access the combined energy of the group. This combined energy amounts to more than the individual energies of each person added up.

A development circle also brings you into regular contact with like-minded, like-hearted people. Even for people who are professional mediums and intuitives, there's often not a lot of opportunity to really talk about what you experience with others who understand. Especially if you don't have a Spiritualist or metaphysical church nearby.

If you're just beginning to develop your gifts, you're going to have a lot of questions and wonderings. Having the community of your development circle can provide a huge amount of relief and reassurance. Even if you're all beginners, you're on the journey together and can give each other support and encouragement.

Another, possibly unexpected, benefit is that you may make friends and develop relationships (preferably platonic ones, but things happen) with some of the people in your circle. In one recent circle I formed, several of the students became great friends and got together with each other for hikes and desserts outside of the circle.

Starting a development circle

Starting a mediumship development circle doesn't have to be complicated or difficult, but there are some things you need to think through and decide before you invite people over and get going.

You'll need to decide whether your circle will be open to new folks each week or stick with the same set of people each time you meet, what you'll focus on, when and where to meet, how long to meet for, how many people to have in your circle, what your expectations are for your circle members, and more.

Use the topics in the following chapters to help you plan what kind of circle you'd like to have and how you want to organize it.

Types of development circles

This book is written primarily for people who want to start a home circle and desire guidance going about doing it successfully. But there are several kinds of development circles, and any kind can use the exercises in this book or the following information about how to set up and run a circle.

The most common types of development circles are home circles and professionally-run circles held by a church, teaching organization or a professional medium.

No matter who's offering or running the circle, it can be either open or closed.

Professionally-run development circles

These kinds of circles are offered and run by a trained professional medium, a church or a teaching organization. These circles often charge a fee, both for the facility use and the professional medium's time and expertise.

Sometimes these kinds of circles are run as an 8-week or 12-week program in mediumship development. Sometimes they are ongoing circles that, essentially, run forever.

Being in a circle led by an experienced medium can be extremely beneficial, as you have someone's guidance in how to connect with Spirit and develop your own mediumship gifts. This is often a useful and crucial step in your unfoldment.

When I first started developing my mediumship skills, I attended classes at my local Spiritualist church, then a church-sponsored circle, then went on to participate in several home circles. When I started working professionally and teaching mediumship, I offered my own mediumship development circle.

Some professionally-run circles may have requirements or pre-requisites you need to meet in order to join them, such as taking a class on mediumship or having a certain amount of prior experience.

Home circles

Home circles are held in the leader's or participants' homes and run by either one person or a rotating group of people. Lots of amazing development happens in home circles. E.W. and M.J. Wallis, pioneers of Spiritualism, refer to home circles as "the soul and salvation of Spiritualism." In their book, *Mediumship Explained*, pages 35-36, they write, "the home circle provides for the proper unfoldment of our mediums" and that it's "often considered the best possible means of discovering the presence of the latent powers of mediumship as well as the simplest and most effective methods of developing them."

Some home circles are run by an experienced medium who leads the circle so they can continue their own growth and share their knowledge. Others are run by a group of students all developing together. Both experiences can be wonderful and useful in developing your mediumship abilities.

One of the best meditations I've ever experienced happened in a home circle I was part of during my initial mediumship development. It's an experience that's stayed with me for decades and still brings me joy when I recall it. My description doesn't do it justice, but I saw each of us in the circle as sunflowers in a field (the sunflower is the symbol of Spiritualism, as they always turn their faces toward the sun, much as we turn toward the light). Essentially, our bodies were the sunflowers' stalks and leaves, and our faces were in the center of each sunflower. Our heads were tilted toward the light and the sunlight, which was the presence of God (or Spirit or the energy of Creation), was flowing into each of us. It was a wonderful, magical experience, feeling so connected to God's love. Because I experienced this during a meditation in a development circle, I was able to share it in a supportive environment with a community who got it.

One of the benefits of a home circle made up of a group of practicing mediums who aren't yet on a professional level is that they share a lot of common ground. You can learn a lot from each other when no one is looking to a leader for the answers. It allows each person in the circle to shine and bring the best of themselves forward.

A benefit for being in a circle run by a professional medium is that you have someone more experienced than you to lean on and learn from. When questions come up, they can answer them. You're also able to receive additional instruction and teaching from the experienced medium which can help with your development, especially if you want to move toward becoming a professional medium yourself and begin seeing clients.

Open circles

Open circles allow anyone who wants to attend to come to any meeting. They're open to new people. There's usually no commitment to regular attendance and people can come as often or as little as they want. They may or may not have a limit on the number of participants.

If you decide to have an open circle, you'll need to determine how many people—minimum and maximum—can attend. Most open circles are run by an experienced medium and held at a rented space, whether that's a church, community center or another neutral location that's not the person's house. This is primarily due to privacy and safety concerns with inviting the general public over to your house.

You'll also need to orient the new people who attend each time as to the nature and purpose of the circle, what to expect and what's expected of them in terms of behavior and confidentiality.

Personally, I'm not a fan of open circles for mediumship development. You get a better blend and buildup of energy in a closed circle. Plus, the participants get to know each other better and build trust. Delivering messages from Spirit to others takes a lot of trust and willingness to be vulnerable and open. I find that's harder for people to do in an open circle than in a closed one.

Open circles can work well if you're presenting a new exercise each week—such as the ones in this book. They also provide fresh loved ones in Spirit to come through as you have different participants who bring their loved ones with them when they attend. This can give your regular attendees more practice with new energy. So they do have benefits, as well.

Closed circles

Closed circles limit who can be in them. They usually have the same people in attendance every time they meet and may have attendance requirements in order to keep the level of energy high enough to achieve communication with Spirit, as well as keeping a harmonious blend of energy among the participants.

Closed circles can have a variety of rules around who can be invited and how. You'll need to decide, as an individual or a group, what those rules or guidelines are for your circle. Some questions to consider are:

- How are new people invited to the circle?
- Are they invited on a probationary period?
- How does the circle decide whether or not they're a good fit?
- How will you deal with personality conflicts and differences that may come up? Highly sensitive people are, after all, sensitive.

Whatever guidelines your circle agrees on need to be communicated and agreed to by all members. You also need to make sure that, when you invite a new person to join your closed circle, that they understand the guidelines for how their admission works. Being able to invite new people in is essential as, no matter how dedicated a group may be when it begins, life happens and people will naturally leave the circle over the course of time. That's OK. Don't fight it when it happens or feel that your circle is necessarily lacking in something or is a failure in any way. It's not only normal, but it's good.

I prefer to sit in a closed circle with a regular group of people attending. It encourages a safe space where people can be vulnerable and build trust between each other and with Spirit. As new people arrive, everyone gets to know them and they become harmonized with the energy of the circle as a whole. However, because the core group of people have been sitting together for a period of time, the addition of a new person every few months doesn't disrupt the circle's overall energy.

What abilities you want to develop

While the bulk of the exercises in this book focus on mental mediumship—developing your intuitive or psychic senses and ability to sense and receive information from people in Spirit—there are a variety of reasons development circles form. Many focus on mental mediumship. But others sit for physical mediumship development, channeling, healing or group meditation.

Choose one main focus for your circle and stick with that. Many forms of physical mediumship take a lot of time and dedication to develop, and most development circles focused on mental mediumship won't have the patience to continue sitting until physical phenomena are produced. A healing circle may sometimes generate mediumship messages, but it's not the circle's focus. And, if your circle wants to sit and simply meditate in company, that's an amazing and worthwhile use of your time as well.

There are some physical mediumship development exercises included at the end of this book, as it can be fun to try, especially if you have an experienced medium in your midst, or as all your individual strengths and talents get stronger. But keep your circle's focus on your main objective and try not to get too distracted.

Circle logistics

There is a certain amount of logistics you need to figure out when you're starting a circle. When to meet, where to meet, how long to meet for, how to set up the room, who will run the circle, and how many people to have in the circle are the main ones.

When to meet

Ideally, your development circle should meet at the same day and time each week. You want to strike the right balance between not meeting too often or too little.

Monthly circles will make it harder to sustain the energy and interest needed to really develop your abilities. Even bi-weekly circles don't quite give you enough consistent practice. Meeting weekly is considered to be the best frequency by many experts and is also my preference, but manage what you can.

Your circle can also meet too frequently. You wouldn't want to have a daily circle, for instance, even if all your circle participants had the time and inclination. Twice a week is still pretty frequent, although in the early stages of my development, I did sit in two separate development circles each week. One focused on physical mediumship and one on mental mediumship.

The best practice: pick one day a week that your circle members can commit to.

You also need to decide on the time of day you're going to meet. Meet at the same time, on the same day each week for consistency—not just in your own schedule, but also so that your Spirit friends and helpers know when to show up.

Mediumship development is a commitment you make with Spirit and your own higher self. Having a consistent schedule in this way not only shows your dedication, but is also great for getting Spirit to quiet down the rest of the time so you can get on with your everyday life.

If Spirit is bothering you throughout your days—or nights, waking you up at 3 a.m.—having a weekly appointment with Spirit for your development allows that to settle down. You're committing to doing the work, Spirit knows you're going to show up and open up to communication, so they don't need to bug you the rest of the time. This really does work.

Where to meet

You also need to decide where you're meeting. This can either be in a physical space in someone's home, a church or other meeting space or in a virtual online space if your circle members are geographically distant from each other.

If you're meeting in a physical location, you need to decide where. Many circles meet in the same place every session and this often works well. You can still have a successful circle if each member takes a turn hosting, though. If you want or need to do that, consider keeping the location to a repeating pattern: e.g., the first week of the month at Joanna's house, the second week at Jill's, the third week at Kelsang's and the fourth week at Theresa's, for instance. If there's a month where your circle's day of the week occurs five times, then pick someone else to host that week, e.g. Rich's house. This helps keep a rhythm to the energy that builds up in each location, and also helps you remember who's house you're supposed to go to each week.

If you're meeting online, you'll need to find the right technology for you. It doesn't need to be overly complicated, though. Zoom, for instance, allows you to host online meetings of up to 100 people for 40 minutes with a free account. Paid accounts, that give you more options, are a reasonable price, currently around $15/month. All each person needs are a laptop, webcam and decent Internet connection.

You may also be able to host a group Google Hangout or group Facetime on your mobile phones, depending on the technology each of the group members has.

Whoever is the most tech savvy will probably want to take the lead on this, get everyone set up to meet online, and send out the invitation so you can meet for your online circle.

How long to meet for

How long should each circle be held for? Somewhere between one and two hours is usual. Sitting for a long period of time can be difficult, but you want to give yourselves enough time to arrive, take a breath and relax, learn something, meditate and share.

I've found that an hour is too short a time to really accomplish much of anything, even though my circles often meditate for only 15-20 minutes during the course of the circle. I'll provide some suggested circle formats a little later on. Personally, I find it difficult to attend events longer than two hours, in terms of both fitting them into my schedule, taking time away from my family, and for my physical stamina and fidgetiness. Somewhere between an hour and 15 minutes and an hour and 45 minutes seems to be the sweet spot.

How to set up the room

There are lots of opinions out there on how to set up a circle that's meeting in a physical location, as opposed to online. You can make it very complicated if you'd like. Or not. It's totally up to you. Please use common sense and your intuition here, rather than a strict set of rules.

Most mediums who write and teach about mediumship development circles seem to agree that, ideally, you're able to set aside a special room dedicated solely to your mediumship work. I've participated in only one circle that met in a dedicated séance room—we were sitting for physical mediumship. Others were in my mentor's home office or in my own office location where I saw clients and taught classes. Most of the circles I've part of have been held in people's living rooms.

In my experience, it doesn't matter. Spirit can figure it out. They know they're welcome to visit when you're sitting in circle, and not when your family is gathered around the TV eating pizza and watching *Mythbusters* on Saturday evenings or playing in virtual reality (these are common occurrences in my living room).

It is a good idea to keep the room reasonably clean and tidy. Get rid of as much clutter as you can—it'll help your own energy and vibration on a daily basis as well—but don't feel it has to be a totally sparse or completely clean room. My house certainly isn't. On the other hand, trying to have a circle in a hoarder's nest will probably cause some difficulties if you're surrounded by an overwhelming amount of stuff.

If the energy in the room feels stagnant, open the windows and doors, smudge with sage or ring a Tibetan chime or singing bowls. It's a good idea to do this on a semi-regular basis, as energy can build up in homes when people argue, get stressed about life in general, or have been ill.

Where should people sit? Allow people to sit wherever they want. Most people will claim one spot and stick with it, sometimes getting territorial about it. Try not to let them get overly attached to one place. It's fine to mix things up. You do not need to have assigned seating. It's also not necessary to seat people in an alternating pattern of male and female, or to try and ascertain if people have a more male or female energy and make sure it's all perfectly balanced. The binary gender model is outdated and you don't need to waste your energy on it.

Honestly, I've never worried about this in any of the circles I've sat in or taught. I've found that it all tends to work out by itself, without need of my intervention.

In terms of lighting, have the room lit to your comfort level. Circles can be held during the day or at night. If it's daylight, you may not want to have sun streaming in through all the windows creating glare, but you also don't need to make the room dim, unless you're sitting for physical mediumship. If it's nighttime, turn on some lamps for a nice soft lighting effect, rather than blaring bright, fluorescent overhead lights. Essentially, you want everyone to feel relaxed and comfortable, so light the room accordingly.

How many people to have in the circle

There are no hard and fast rules on the number of people that should be in a circle together. There are some logical limits, especially if you're meeting in a physical space.

I haven't found circles to be successful with less than four or five members. This is for two reasons. One is that you need a certain amount of energy to build up over the course of your circle meetings. It's true that you could have just one partner and have access to more energy than your own. But it's not quite the same. The second reason is that, due to the vagaries of life, when you have fewer than four or five people in a circle, there are going to be weeks when one or two of them can't attend, leaving you with just one other person. If you're content to simply sit in meditation or try a partner exercise that week, that's fine. But it tends to diminish the overall energy and momentum of the group.

Conversely, you don't want to have such a large group that it's unmanageable. This is true in an obvious we-can't-fit-everyone-in-the-room way as well as in an energetic way. If you have too many people in your circle, you may never feel particularly close as a group. Plus, because of the number of people, there's likely to be less consistent attendance. This is true even for an online group where you don't have to find enough chairs for everyone to sit in.

How many is too many? I'd say more than 13 is too many.

That means you want to aim for somewhere between five and 11 people, with seven or eight often being considered the ideal. In the end, you do what works for you and your group. If you have five people who meet consistently, week in and week out, that's great. If you find a dozen other people who mesh well together and keep showing up to develop, and a large enough physical location if you're meeting in person, that's excellent, too.

Setting guidelines and expectations

If you've read any of my other books, taken any classes with me or even watched my YouTube videos, you probably know I'm big on boundaries. Setting expectations for your circle is a great way to establish boundaries from the start.

This means there are certain things you want to decide on—such as what regular attendance entails—and things you want to simply set ground rules about.

It may seem like overkill, but it's worthwhile to put together a document with your circle's guidelines and expectations that all members have to read and agree to. You don't necessarily need signed forms, but stating how the circle will operate puts everyone on the same page and gives people something to refer back to if needed.

I've included a sample guidelines document at the end of this chapter.

Food and socializing

A couple of expectations to begin with are about food and socializing.

Circle time is not time to eat lunch or dinner. Some circles like to end with a light snack and a cup of tea. This is fine, but don't start your circle with food or let people eat during the circle. I've made this mistake myself.

In one of my first home circles, we rotated between attendees' houses and we began each circle with a little socializing time. This can work, and worked well for a while, but then we started to get a bit too focused on the food and chatting.

I'll confess this is partly my fault as I'd learned how to make bacon-wrapped scallops and, after serving them at a dinner party, I decided to make them the next time I hosted the circle. They were admittedly delicious, but we all ate too much and didn't have a very good experience in our meditation or message work as we were all stuffed and sleepy. I was then banned from making bacon-wrapped scallops ever again and we began to focus more on why we were meeting together in the first place: to develop our mediumship skills.

Another thing you want to avoid is talking about politics or areas of life that don't pertain to the circle and its purpose. It's great for circle members to get to know each other on a personal level and is one of the many benefits for a mediumship development circle. But that shouldn't be happening too much during the circle itself.

We all have frustrations in life and people often come from work or from dealing with family members, but try and leave that at the door as much as humanly possible. Whatever you do, don't start talking about politics, social media or healthcare.

If people want to share those parts of their lives, they definitely can, after and outside of your circle. Go out to coffee or dessert afterwards—several of my students have enjoyed going to a local patisserie after circle—or meet for a hike or a playdate with the kids. It doesn't belong during your circle time and will bring the energy down. You don't want that.

Regular attendance

If you have a closed circle, every member of your circle needs to make the commitment to attend regularly. What's regular attendance? I tell my students they should plan to be there every week unless they just can't make it. At a minimum, they should be there at least three out of four weeks. Without sounding harsh, if your life can't accommodate that commitment, a closed circle is probably not the right thing for you right now.

If your circle is open, then people are free to attend as they please.

One note about expectations and how they differ with closed and open circles: if you have a closed circle, you should only need to go over these expectations at the beginning and when new members are added. If you have an open circle, you'll need to make these expectations clear in the event description—presuming you're advertising it on social media, flyers or church bulletins—as well as at the start of each circle.

Punctuality

Punctuality is as important as regular attendance. Having someone habitually arrive late disrupts the flow of the circle and is disrespectful. You need to get your life in order and be able to leave it at the door, arrive on time and allow your energy to blend with the others in the group.

If you're going to be late, let the circle leader or others in the group know, so they can wait to begin the circle proper until you arrive. Some circles create a little leeway in the start time by beginning the circle with a short discussion about the spiritual and mediumship experiences they've had in the past week. This allows you some time to settle in before starting the meditation. You can read more about that in the circle format section.

Starting a circle – Setting guidelines and expectations

Behavioral expectations

In addition to some of the logistical expectations, you need to set behavioral expectations and boundaries as well. What does this mean? Well, how people interact with each other in this sacred space matters. For the most part, people are going to be kind to each other and open to what unfolds. But, if you're leading the group or are part of forming a circle, it's important to ensure that people are being open-hearted and open-minded toward each other and what transpires during your circle meetings.

As a Spiritualist minister, I follow the principles of Spiritualism, and simplify my expectations to:

- Spirit, the force of life, is everywhere, always, in nature, in each other, in ourselves.
- Treat other people as you'd like to be treated.
- Take responsibility for yourself, for where you are in your life and where you're going.
- People make mistakes. That's OK. Give them the benefit of the doubt.
- Be kind, always.

Confidentiality

What happens during your circles is confidential. It's not secret or hidden, but it's not something to be shared with other people outside of the circle, or even talked or gossiped about among other circle members.

You need this confidentiality so that people feel comfortable in being open to the growth that occurs—on both a personal and mediumship level—during your time together in circle. People will share things with circle members and have deeply moving and meaningful experiences that they're not ready to share with the outside world. Having the trust of your circle members is essential in this growth.

Attitude

Developing your mediumship and spiritual gifts is an undertaking of unknown length. Some people are going to seem to develop quicker than others. Some will be more confident and willing to give out the messages and information they receive. Others will be reticent and wary of the trust required. We all come from different places and are walking different paths. It's OK.

Take care with your attitude toward yourself and the other participants. Don't be competitive. This is a cooperative activity. As the Morris Pratt Institute Educational Course on Modern Spiritualism puts it, "A competitive attitude among the sitters seeking unfoldment is destructive. Each one will unfold in his or her own way. There should be no rivalry, but rather a strong desire and perfect willingness for the spirit power to manifest through whomever it wishes, however possible."

If you surrender your growth to the path of your highest good, you'll unfold in the perfect way, in the perfect timing for you. You're the only person who can live your life and walk your particular path.

Hygiene and perfumes

This may seem like an odd item to include in setting expectations for your circle. But rather than people coming to circle unwashed and unkempt, the opposite is more likely to be true.

Starting a circle – Setting guidelines and expectations

If you get a group of energetically sensitive people together, more than likely, at least one of them will be sensitive to fragrances and perfumes. I've found it a common thing among mediums. Wearing a lot of scent isn't good for anyone, but it can make chemically sensitive people truly ill. Therefore, making it a rule that no one should wear any perfume, and preferably not use perfumed body products or laundry detergent and fabric softener is a good way to go.

Finding circle participants

Now that we've covered the various logistics and decisions about what kind of circle to have, when and where it will meet, how long you'll meet for and how many people you want to have, you need to actually get a group of people together. (If you've already got an interested group of potential circle members, you can skip this bit.)

How do you find like-minded and like-hearted folks with similar goals? Whether you're looking to join a development circle or start one, in person or online, here are some ideas to help you get together with the right folks.

Spiritualist and metaphysical churches

First look for a Spiritualist or metaphysical church in your area. Depending where you are, churches that teach and practice mediumship may be called Spiritualist or metaphysical. Not all metaphysical churches, such as Centers for Spiritual Living and Unity, teach mediumship, but some are open to it and may be a good resource to post a flyer or find others with similar interests.

Many Spiritualist churches run mediumship development circles as part of their teaching programs. You may be able to join an already running circle or meet others who are already part of a home circle or want to join or start one.

New age, pagan and metaphysical stores

Some stores that are focused on new age, new thought, pagan, Wiccan, occult and metaphysics may offer mediumship instruction and circles. If not, they're a good place to meet people with similar interests.

Talk to the proprietor of any such stores in your area to see if they have classes or a development circle or can help you find people interested in being part of one. You may be able to put up a flyer with information about your proposed circle or they might be willing to put a notice in their newsletter.

Independent bookstores, rock shops, food co-ops and other likely spots

Not to stereotype people who want to develop their mediumship abilities, but many of us have similar additional interests, such as supporting our local community, reading, eating health food and being drawn to sparkly things from the Earth.

Many independent bookstores, organic food stores and similar small-businesses have bulletin boards covered with flyers offering workshops, classes and events in your local community. Look at these bulletin boards. See if something catches your interest. Is there someone doing an All Message Service or gallery reading event? Is there someone who offers a monthly channeling and meditation? Go to those events and talk to the organizers. They can help you find your tribe.

You can also put up your own flyers in these spots to advertise your circle.

Your own friends

Don't ask all your friends and family, but check in with the ones who you know are intuitive and open. Maybe they'll want to be part of your circle. Or maybe they know people they can connect you with.

Nextdoor neighborhood app

If you want to join or create a local group, take a look at Nextdoor, a phone app and website that lets you connect with people in your neighborhood and the ones adjacent to where you live. It's a useful way of finding out what's going on locally.

You can see if there's anything already going on in your area and, if there's not, put the feelers out to see if anyone in your nearby area is interested.

Meetup.com

Meetup is another site that helps you learn about what's going on in your area. You can search by interest subjects, such as mediumship, and see what comes up.

If you want to start your own circle, especially if you want it to be an open circle, or at least have the first few meetings open, creating your own event on Meetup is an easy way to find people. I ran my first open, public circle this way and consistently found people to attend. It's a good way to get the word out.

Facebook

Facebook can be a useful way to connect with people both in your local area and to find an online development circle. You can search groups by keywords and you're likely to find a plethora of groups focused on mediumship, psychic skills, paranormal phenomena and related subjects.

Some areas have local or regional groups. For example, there's a metaphysical group focused on the Pacific Northwest, the area in which I live. There are also national, international and even more local groups.

Once you've found some groups that look all right and you have a good feeling about, read their guidelines, request to join them and post about what you're looking for.

Online directories

I haven't had much success finding reliable online directories of mediumship development circles, whether they meet in person or online.

Here's what I've found at the time of publishing this book.

James Van Praagh: http://www.vanpraagh.com/development-circle/

Konstanza Morning Star, an NSAC certified medium and the author of *Medium: a step-by-step guide to communicating with the spirit world*, offers an online circle: www.silverspringoflight.com.

You can also try typing phrases like "psychic mediumship development circle" into your favorite search engine.

Circle checklist

Now that you've thought through all the considerations that go into creating and running a development circle, here's a checklist to help you keep track of what kind of circle you'll have and all its variables.

Before you begin your circle (before you even start looking for participants, perhaps) you should know what you want for your circle in each of these areas.

- Type of circle (open or closed)
- What you're developing (mental mediumship, healing, physical mediumship, meditation)
- When you meet (e.g. Mondays at 7 p.m.)
- Length of each circle meeting
- Location where you're meeting
- Number of participants
- Guidelines and expectations document
- How new people are introduced and invited
- How new members are decided to be included or not

Circle Guidelines example document

A group of my students formed a mediumship development circle and put together this document for their circle's guidelines. Many thanks to Kelsang Drime for allowing me to reprint this. I've added my comments as notes.

Soul Connections Mediumship Circle Guidelines

The following guidelines facilitate the functional operation of Soul Connections Mediumship Development Circle.

Purpose of the circle:

Mediumship development circles have two primary purposes: 1) to develop the psychic senses, and 2) to "Sit in the Power." The primary focus of Soul Connections Mediumship Circle will be on Sitting in the Power. *Sitting in the Power is a daily practice for serious students of mediumship.*

(Note: This states the purpose of this particular circle.)

Attendance expectations

Regular attendance and participation in a development circle is essential for any serious student of mediumship. In a closed Circle, it is mandatory that participants attend each week.

Obviously, there may be emergencies or situations that come up beyond the participant's control. However, it is extremely important that once the commitment to attend is made that it is kept. Consistent attendance is essential as the absence of one member from a closed circle changes the entire chemistry of the group and may potentially affect the results in a negative way.

(Note: This section states what the participation requirement or expectation is.)

Adding members

It is suggested that circle leaders interview potential participants prior to beginning the circle for the purpose of determining their level of experience, commitment, and potential issues—personal or professional—which might affect their ability to attend regularly.

Since harmony is essential for success in any group, the circle leader needs to assess the potential participant energetically in terms of their compatibility with other participants. A sincere individual will still adversely affect the results of a circle if their chemistry is not harmonious with the others in the group.

Circle leaders must trust their intuition in such situations and respond accordingly.

(Note: This explains how new people are added to the group and what qualities the circle leader is looking for—their level of experience to make sure it's in line with the rest of the participants, their level of commitment to regular attendance and anything that might interfere with that, and their general energetic harmony with the rest of the Circle members.

This last one can be tricky, which is why your circle leader needs to trust themselves and their own intuition.)

Before the Circle Commences:

- Please, if due to illness or unavoidable absence, you are unable to attend the circle, or you are going to be late, let the other members know in advance.

- Please familiarize yourself with the "Sitting in the Power" meditation practice prior to attending the circle.

- Please set your intention to become more aware of your Soul and connect with your source on the day of the Circle. Avoid negativity and gossip and concentrate on being more positive and empowering.

- It is good to eat a light meal an hour and a half or two before the session. Too much food weighs down the physical body with an active digestive system and makes it difficult for the participant to achieve a deeper altered-state. Great amounts of psychic force are used for the circle and the energy is generated from the solar plexus center. An active digestive system makes this harder to accomplish and potentially gets in the way of proper attunement. Of course, most people would be uncomfortable on a completely empty stomach, which is why it is important to eat a light meal beforehand.

- Alcohol and other intoxicants, consumed even in small amounts on the day of the meeting, must be completely avoided as they pollute the vibrations and create disharmonious conditions.

- Cleaning the body and wearing fresh clothes externally brings cleanliness into the circle both physically and subtly as the clothes worn in daily life absorb denser material energies.

- Please refrain from wearing perfume, cologne, essential oils and body lotions with strong scents as they can distract the mind.

- Participants should attempt to arrive at the circle around 10-15 minutes before the scheduled session is to begin.

Starting a circle – Circle guidelines document

Arriving harried or stressed due to the anxiety of trying to get there on time should be avoided. An early arrival allows adequate time to relax and settle into the right state of mind. Anxiety or mental tenseness does the exact opposite. Problems of a personal nature also need to be left outside the door, although, realistically, this may not always be humanly possible.

- Keeping this point in mind, it is beneficial for creating the right mental state for the leader to conduct a short healing meditation to relax the physical body and rid the mind of unnecessary anxieties and problems.

- Please come to the circle with an open mind with joy and gratitude, letting go of any expectations of what might happen.

- Please use the bathroom, if necessary, prior to arrival or before the circle commences.

- Please turn your cellphone off once you arrive.

- Please bring paper and pen/pencil for any notes.

- The seating arrangement of the group is important. In traditional circles, it was appropriate to alternate between male and females as this was thought to be conducive to the flow of energy between participants. What matters most is that the participants are dedicated, patient, and compatible. Energetic harmony is an absolute necessity. Once you have been placed or have intuitively decided upon your seat within the circle, this is your 'assigned' seat during every circle.

(Note: These are this particular circle's expectations before the circle starts. It covers many of the common expectations around punctuality, hygiene and the like. In my own circles, I let people sit wherever they want, trusting they'll be naturally drawn to the best area for them to sit in. Human nature also seems to cause people to want to sit in the same seat every time.)

After the Circle Commences:

- Once the circle starts, unless requested, do not get up or move about. Stay in your chair at all times as sudden movement may disrupt the delicate energies that have built up.

- Do not touch other circle participants after the opening prayer. This creates an energetic shock to both participants.

- Please respect the other members of the circle and those from the spirit world who take the time and effort to work with you. Retain confidentiality at all times in terms of what has taken place in the circle with other participants. Do not gossip or discuss intimate details of others in the circle outside of the group. Comparing oneself to another and/or developing jealousy or envy is a sure path to misery…so don't.

- Please remember the best progress is slow and steady. It is not a race and there are no shortcuts in the development of mediumship.

- Please always ask for the highest good of all.

The admission of new Circle participants:

- The Soul Connections Mediumship Development Circle is limited to 9 physical participants, unless otherwise agreed upon by all participants or space allows. This is because our meeting space and time are concentrated.

- Any new participant must be invited and sponsored by an existing participant of the circle.

- Any new participant must be evaluated prior to participation in the circle. This allows the circle to evaluate their level of experience, commitment, and potential issues, personal or professional, which might affect their ability to attend regularly.

- Any new participant will be probationary for a 1-month period. This allows for both the existing circle participants and the probationary participant to determine whether sufficient energetic harmony is maintained to allow the probationary participant's continued participation.

- At the end of the 1-month probationary period, the existing circle participants must anonymously vote to determine the probationary participant's continued participation.

- In the event of an even vote, the facilitator must determine the probationary participant's continued participation by throw-of-dice—an even number allows their continued participation and an odd number will not.

- Both existing circle participants and any new participant must understand this process is not personal but, rather, is intended to preserve the energetic harmony of the circle as well as allow for the personal development of all parties involved.

Running a circle

Now let's get into the nuts and bolts of actually running your circle. This includes topics such as who's going to run the circle, the things that may come up during the process of running it, and an outline for some suggested formats of what you actually do during your time together.

Your circle has to be run by someone. It's not enough to just get a group of people willing to meet together at a certain day and time. Someone has to be the organizing force behind it. And someone has to lead people through the activities that occur during the circle.

This doesn't necessarily have to be the same person, or even just one person. For instance, you might be the person organizing the circle's creation and sending out invitations or reminders, but one of the other members may have more experience and enjoy leading a group. Or perhaps your circle decides to rotate leaders, with each person bringing an exercise, topic or meditation to work with each week. It's totally up to you.

Roles

The circle organizer, facilitator and participants each have different roles. (The organizer and facilitator can be the same person, and often is, in the case of an experienced medium offering a home circle.) This is also true when you rotate the role of facilitator among participants.

Organizer

The circle organizer is responsible for making sure everyone has agreed to the circle's guidelines and expectations, that people know when and where to show up, and for making sure the room you meet in has what it needs—enough chairs and adequate heating and cooling, for example.

Participants

The participants are responsible for showing up and behaving themselves. They need to come with good attitudes, be open and be in integrity. During the circle, they need to be present, do their best to connect with Spirit and trust themselves, participate in the exercises and give out the messages they receive.

Facilitator or leader

The facilitator or leader holds the space for the group. Because of this they usually don't get to go as deeply into the meditations as everyone else, as they need to pay attention to the energy of the group and the time. They keep things moving along, while leading the group.

What is holding the space or the energy for a group? It's being a healing presence, holding space energetically, being totally present and available to the people you're with. That doesn't necessarily mean directing and teaching. Sometimes a facilitator will let things unfold as they need to. It means being an open heart and grounding force (and sometimes a battery) for the other participants, so they can learn and move forward in their development.

The facilitator can also get a lot of healing, learning and unfoldment while taking on this role, but it is a different experience than that of the other participants.

For simplicity, the exercises in this book often refer to the "circle leader." This means the person leading that specific exercise, whether or not they're the ones organizing or leading the circle as a whole, or just that specific exercise.

Format

There are several formats that mediumship development circles often take. In general, they include an invocation, a period of learning about an aspect of mediumship, meditation, sharing and closing.

Invocation and closing

You should always open and close your circle with a brief prayer. These can be simple and short, as few people like to listen to prayers that go on and on.

Here's an invocation I often use in my circles:

Gracious Spirit, Infinite Intelligence, thank you for bringing us together today so that we may learn and grow together, in a nurturing, supportive circle. Help us to have the courage to give out the messages we receive, knowing that only the highest and best good comes to us. Our doors are open. And so it is.

To close the circle, I use a short prayer along the lines of:

Spirit, thank you for the learning we shared together today, for the love and laughter and healing. We trust and know you will be with us and guide our steps until we meet again. Our doors are closed.

Learning and exercises

The learning or class portion can be a topic presented by the facilitator or it can be an exercise you all do together. Most mediumship development circles like to work on developing different areas of mental mediumship—such as understanding and opening the chakras, or developing the phases of mental mediumship—spending a week or two on each area.

The exercises in this book have a brief section on that specific aspect of mediumship—clairvoyance, clairaudience, etc.—followed by exercises to help you develop it for yourself.

Meditation

Every mediumship development circle should involve meditation. Meditation allows you to settle your own energy and harmonize with the energy of the group, creating something larger than your individual selves.

The practice of meditation also develops your capacity for mental focus and for being in the present moment—both of which you need to be able to get into the flow state of receiving messages from Spirit.

Some circles like to begin with a short 5-to-10-minute meditation to get everyone settled and present in the space together, allowing their energy to harmonize. Others only meditate as part of the exercise for the day. Or you can do both. There isn't a right or wrong way to go about it. There just has to be a period of meditation at some point.

Your circle may work best to have the meditation first, before the exercise or learning part of the circle program. Or you may find you prefer it after everyone has had a chance to share and talk about their experiences related to mediumship since you last met.

In terms of the meditation itself, you can have a silent meditation, a self-guided meditation to soothing music, or a guided meditation. Guided visualizations can be very useful, especially if your group as a whole or some of its new members are in the stage of learning to meditate. The visualizations give your mind something to focus on.

As far as the length of your meditation period(s), you can meditate for 5 to 10 minutes to settle the group's energy, and should meditate for at least 15 minutes to prepare yourself for doing message work. Many circles meditate for 15 to 30 minutes during the main meditation portion if they're not doing another development exercise.

Sharing

One of the benefits of a mediumship development circle, other than the combined energies of those present, is the ability to share with others what you experience. Not only does this build community, it decreases your own sense of loneliness and isolation. Let's face it, you're probably not talking to lots of people about your mediumship experiences. You could probably do with some understanding spiritual community.

Sharing your experiences with others of like mind and heart also gives you the opportunity to get feedback. You'll be surprised to learn how many other members of your circle saw something similar in their meditation, or got the same color during a meditation in which you worked on sensing the dominant color of each of your circle members. This kind of feedback is incredibly affirming—both for the person giving it and the person receiving it!

If the purpose of the meditation was to sit for messages for the other circle members, the sharing time is when you give out those messages. Summon your courage and give them. Your circle is a safe place for you to develop and grow. Part of that development is trusting yourself and your connection with Spirit enough to share what you receive. Sharing completes the circuit and tells your guides and the people in Spirit that you're hearing (or seeing or smelling or whatever) them, which means they'll keep giving you more information next time.

Example circle formats

Here's an example of a circle format for a circle that lasts 1 ½ hours and does a meditation first, followed by sharing or a teaching exercise.

11:00 am: Circle members arrive, take off their coats and use the bathroom if necessary, then take their seat and begin the process of relaxation/concentration.

11:10 am: The facilitator invites Spirit into the space with a prayer of invocation as the members hold hands.

11:15 am: Circle members do a Sitting in the Power meditation, allowing their individual souls to blend with the other members of the circle and Spirit for 15 to 30 minutes.

11:30 am/11:45 am to 12:15 pm: Discussion about everyone's feelings and experiences within the circle, or members engage in a predetermined development exercise.

12:15 pm: The facilitator closes the circle with a prayer of gratitude. The circle members usually have a hot drink or some form of light refreshments, if provided, to restore energy and vitality.

12:30 pm: Each member cleans the room, collects their belongings and departs.

Here's an example format for a circle in which there's some general sharing at the beginning, followed by a teaching time and a meditation for messages.

Running a circle – Format

11:00 am: Circle members arrive.

11:05 am: Circle members catch up on the week sharing their experiences since they last met.

11:15 am: The facilitator opens the circle with an invocation, then goes one of the exercises from this book or a predetermined teaching related to mediumship.

11:45 am: The circle meditates for messages.

12:00 pm: Members share their experiences from the meditation.

12:30 pm: The facilitator closes the circle and members collect their things and depart.

You're free to modify this in whatever way you need to for your own circle's needs and goals. You may also find that you differ slightly from week to week. For instance, if you were to go through each of the exercises in this book, the first week you might learn about clairvoyance, then have a meditation to connect with Spirit and your own higher self. The second week, you'd do an exercise on sending and receiving images during the learning portion of the circle, then have a meditation to connect with Spirit. The third week you'd perhaps to the meditation first, concentrating on the photographs you've each brought in, and then have an extended sharing time to give each other the impressions you came up with.

Be flexible. It's good to have a general outline of what to expect, but be flexible and listen to your intuition.

Connecting with Spirit

One of the goals of mediumship development is learning to connect with Spirit. Some people call this Sitting in the Power. I like to call it connecting in with your own divinity, as it's through your connection with your inner spark of divinity that you're able to connect with the energy of others in Spirit and your guides.

Whenever you begin to work with Spirit, whether you're in a development circle or working on your own, you should open your energy to Spirit and set your intention. When you're finished, you need to close yourself to communication from Spirit. To do this, you need to understand boundaries.

This chapter is about all of these things: opening and closing the circle with prayer, setting intention and boundaries, connecting to Spirit through linking in with your divine self, and blending your energy with Spirit.

Opening and closing the circle

Opening your circle with an invocation is the easiest way to get everyone ready and open to Spirit. A short prayer creates a ritual, giving everyone a sense of safety and familiarity and allowing them to relax into the circle. It doesn't need to be long or complicated.

You use this invocation to set your intent, open your doors to Spirit and lead into your meditation.

Here's a prayer I often use for my circles:

Gracious Spirit, Infinite Intelligence,

Thank you for bringing us together here today for our time of meditation and connection. We know that we each receive only our highest and best good as we open to and connect with Spirit.

As we receive messages for others today, give us the courage to give them out.

With this, our doors are open.

And so it is.

Closing your circle at the end is equally as important. This signals to each of you and to Spirit that your time of meditation and connection is over. It's another ritual that prepares you for re-entry into the world.

A closing prayer could go like this:

Gracious Spirit, Infinite Intelligence.

Thank you for our time together today, for the messages given and received, for the growth and learning we've experienced.

Connecting with Spirit– Opening and closing the circle

May the light of Spirit shine upon the path of our highest good until we return to be together again.

Our doors are closed.

And so it is.

Setting your intention and boundaries

Setting your intention, so you receive only the highest good and have a pleasant experience connecting with Spirit, is actually a straightforward process.

You set your intention at the beginning of your opening prayer when you ask for the highest good of everyone. Because of the natural laws that govern mediumship (read my book, *Led by Light, book 1* for more on those), when you set your intention, it makes it so.

It's important that everyone in your circle is on the same page about this. You must each want only your highest good and the highest good of everyone involved. This means that folks who are there because, perhaps, they want to get spooked by Spirit aren't a good fit.

Boundaries and intention go hand in hand. You need to have good boundaries when you work with energy, especially if you go on to give public or professional readings. The people who visit mediums to connect with loved ones in Spirit are grieving, which makes them vulnerable. This means you, as a medium, need to be in integrity and have solid boundaries in place.

When you're developing your mediumship skills, boundaries are more about what you're willing to let in from Spirit. This connects with setting your intention as, once you state that you're only interested in receiving your highest good, your boundaries ensure that's all you'll let in. If you sense anything that doesn't feel good to you, don't let it in—much like you wouldn't let someone you don't trust into your home. Don't let energy that doesn't feel right to you into your energetic area.

Connecting with your divine self

To get messages, you need to be connected to Spirit. You need to tune into the energy of your guides and folks in Spirit. In order to do this, your own energy needs to be clear and quiet, so you can focus on what's being communicated to and through you.

The reason mediumship development circles have a period of meditation is to accomplish both of these things: to quiet yourself enough to be able to hear Spirit and to get into the place where you can truly connect with the energy and understand the communication coming through.

Some mediumship teachers recommend an exercise most commonly called Sitting in the Power, in which you generate your own internal power and then blend your energy with Spirit. Some teachers, like mine, just called it meditating.

Different teachers have varying methods for doing this. One I like is what Konstanza Morningstar describes in her book, *Medium: A Step-by-Step Guide to Communicating with the Spirit World* (pages 56-59).

The overall idea is that you allow yourself to relax into meditation, while staying in your body and becoming aware of your own internal energy or light. You allow this light to be fueled by Spirit and to grow.

If you prefer, you can imagine a source of energy or light greater than you—such as God, Christ light, Source, Gaia, etc.—blending in with your energy. Personally, I prefer to imagine myself plugged directly into the Source energy outlet, able to absorb and drink in as much as I need, rather than seeing it as a separate energy from me that overlaps or overshadows me. But do what works for you.

Here's a similar guided meditation I use with my students. For your circle, have one person lead the rest of the group in this meditation.

Connecting with the divine guided meditation

- Set your intent with an invocation:

Gracious Spirit, we're here today to connect with our Source energy and know we do so with love and for our highest good. And so it is.

- Get into a comfortable, but alert/upright meditation position.
- With your eyes open, take 3 deep breaths, in through your nose and out through your mouth. Release each breath with an *Ahhhhhh*.
- Close your eyes and allow your breathing to return to its natural pattern.
- Notice the sensation of the weight of your body sitting in the chair, your feet on the floor, your hands in your lap.
- Notice any smells in the air, the sensation of air on your skin, and the sounds in the room around you.
- Scan your body, starting with your head and steadily moving down toward your feet. Notice, but don't analyze.
- Allow your body to relax, while staying within it. If your awareness begins to leave your body, bring it back to your breath.

- Bring your awareness to within your body—to the divine spark within you. This may be in your pelvis, your solar plexus, your heart, your third eye or crown. Wherever your attention goes to is just right. If it shifts, that's OK, too.
- Begin breathing into this area of your body. Allow it to soften and open to your life-giving breath.
- Just as your breath gives your body oxygen, it also fans the flame of your divinity. As you exhale, imagine Spirit energy filling you and making the light within you brighter and brighter. As you inhale, imagine oxygen entering your lungs, giving your body life.
- Exhale, the light within you expanding and opening, filling with life-sustaining spiritual energy.
- Inhale, your body being fed the oxygen it needs.
- Imagine breathing in and out of this part of your body, feeling its power gradually grow. Allow the light within you to grow and grow until it becomes a beacon of light. It may want to spill out into the world around you. Let it.
- You can imagine it spreading from the room you're in, across the street, throughout your neighborhood, throughout the city, state, country, world, out into the cosmos.
- This is your light. It's fueled by your connection with Spirit, with the energy of all that is. It is yours.
- You don't need to make any effort here, let it flow as it wants to naturally flow.
- If you connect with the idea of God, Christ or another master teacher, imagine their light blending with yours.

That pure energy is attracted to your bright light and envelopes you in pure love. Allow it to nourish and sustain you.

- Surrender to this feeling of being embraced by light and love and being fully plugged into to the universal energy source.
- Be in this moment.
- After several minutes: become aware again of your breathing, feel the sensation of weight of your body pressed into the chair you're sitting in, the sensation of air on your skin, become aware of your body and your breath, and the room around you. Wiggle your fingers and toes and open your eyes.

Mediumship development circle exercises

Now for the exercises themselves. The following chapters are grouped together by the area of skill you're developing, e.g. clairvoyance (intuitive or psychic seeing), clairaudience (intuitive or psychic hearing), etc.

Many of the exercises were originally written with the understanding that the circle meets in the same physical location. Everyone is together in the same room, and does the exercises either together as a circle or in pairs as noted in each exercise.

However, many circles meet online. Their members are physically distant, but are in the same virtual place during the circle, connected via webcam. I've offered adaptations to each exercise for online circles. Many can be adapted without much—or any—fuss.

There are a few exercises, the ones where you have to physically exchange objects, for instance, that can't be easily adapted to an online circle. But if you figure out a way to do it, go for it (and let me know, so I can update this book and give you credit).

You can try any of the exercises, in any order.

Pick one that appeals to you, or that your circle members have expressed an interest in learning about and give it a try.

You can use the introductory text at the beginning of each chapter as a learning or discussion tool, then move on to an exercise on that topic. For a deeper understanding of each of the clairsenses, see my book, *Led by Light: A Medium's Guide to Developing Your Intuitive and Psychic Senses, book 2*.

However you organize your circle—with one consistent leader or rotating facilitators—have one person responsible for reading through the exercise ahead of time and being prepared to lead it.

For some exercises, the instructions are step-by-step directions the leader can explain to the group before starting the exercise as use for reference as they go through it. Some exercises need to be led throughout. For others, the circle leader will need to guide the group in and out of the exercise. A general script to do this follows.

Beginning the exercises

Many of the exercises in this book begin their instruction with: *Get into a quiet and comfortable state*, or *Begin in a light state of meditation*, or something similar.

Your circle might already be quite comfortable and capable of doing this without any prompting, but I've generally led my circles into such a meditative state with the following script. Feel free to adapt it to your needs.

- Sit straight and upright in your chair. Relax your shoulders and jaw.
- Begin with 3 cleansing breaths, in through your nose, and out through your mouth with an *Aaahhh*.
- With the third exhalation, allow your eyes to close and your breathing to return to its normal rhythm.

- Take a moment here to bring yourself into the present moment.

- Become aware of the sensation of your body, the weight of your bottom in the seat, your feet on the floor, your hands in your lap.

- Become aware of the sounds in the room around you. Don't resist them, just notice them.

- Become aware of your breath, going in and out of your body. If you find your mind wandering, come back to your breath, feeling it in your body as you inhale and exhale.

From here, you can proceed through the rest of the exercise, whether you're guiding the circle in an activity or continuing the script in the exercise.

Ending the exercises

It's also very helpful to guide your circle out of the exercise. This helps people know when the exercise is ending and it gently brings their awareness back into the room, and into the present.

Sometimes your circle members will wander off in their minds during the exercise and not really be present for it. Sometimes they'll even fall asleep.

By having a standard script that brings them back, you're allowing their energy to recombine with the group and their awareness to come back gently. If you've ever been in a deep meditation, especially if you're awareness has traveled outside of your body, and come back suddenly, you know how jarring and unpleasant that can feel. Avoid that, if you can, by giving your circle members a way to gracefully reenter the circle.

I usually use the following:

- As we end the exercise, it's time for your awareness to come back into the present.
- Allow yourself to become aware of the sounds in the room around you.
- Feel the sensation of your body, of your breath going in and out of your lungs.
- Feel the weight of your body in the seat you're sitting in, your feet on the floor, and your hands in your lap.
- Notice any sensation of air on your skin or smells in the room.
- Bring yourself into the present.
- Wiggle your fingers and toes and, when you're ready, open your eyes.

General mediumship development exercises

Most of the exercises in this book focus on specific aspects of mental mediumship and developing the clairsenses—claircognizance, clairvoyance, clairaudience, clairgustance, clairalience and clairsentience.

The exercises in this first chapter don't focus on any particular clairsenses, but are a good starting point for general mediumship development.

You may find that some of the information that comes through in the beginning stages of your development may feel more psychic or intuitive than mediumistic. You may connect to general energy and impressions about the person, rather than their loved ones in Spirit.

This is OK. It's normal.

Some mediumship teachers are against this kind of information coming through but, in terms of a development circle, it's a reasonable and normal place to start. You'll get to the point of connecting with folks in Spirit and bringing through evidential information from them.

A huge part of your successful unfoldment is simply trusting yourself enough to share what you get.

In fact, many of the exercises in this book don't focus solely on connecting with loved ones in Spirit. They focus on developing different aspects of your abilities, which will then allow you to receive accurate and useful information when you

General mediumship development exercises

do connect in with someone's loved one in Spirit. You need to develop these aspects of your abilities first in order to be able to give messages.

Think of your development circle as your safe training ground, where you learn the moves and techniques that you can then use during readings. You don't need to go at full speed. Just start from where you are right now and go from there at whatever speed feels natural to you.

Billet readings

Billet readings are sometimes done at mediumship events, where each person in the audience writes down a question on a piece of paper and places it in a bowl. The medium then chooses one paper at a time, connects with information about it and delivers the message, before unfolding the paper and reading the question.

This exercise is similar, except you'll each have someone else's question to get information about during a meditation period.

How to do the exercise

Get enough slips of paper and pens for each member of your circle, as well as a bowl to put them in.

- Each person writes down a question about their life that's been on their heart and mind. It's best if the question relates to them directly and isn't a general question about life or the nature of reality. It's fine if the question is related to someone in Spirit.

- Fold the slip of paper a couple of times, so you can't read what's written on it, and place it in a bowl.

- Pass the bowl around the circle, with each person hopefully taking someone else's paper. Don't look at what's written on it! Just hold it quietly in your hand. Occasionally, someone will end up with their own question, but it's rare. However, they won't know it, because they won't read the question before meditating, so they can still get good and accurate information, unbiased by their opinions and emotions.

- Once each person has a slip of paper, go into a meditation for 7-10 minutes.

- During that time, relax into the energy of the paper and the question it contains. Allow impressions to come into your awareness: images, feelings, thoughts, sounds, smells, tastes. Don't judge them or even try and interpret them necessarily. Notice them and note them.

- It's OK to ask questions of your guides or the person in Spirit who may be connected to the question or the person asking it. You can ask for clarity, but try to do so without too much interpretation on your part.

- After the meditation, go around the circle, one by one, and share what you got. After you've shared, read the question and find out who the message was for.

Online

Because each person doesn't see the question they get before they meditate on it, there's no good way to do this online while keeping the question blind.

If you're OK seeing the question, everyone could message the circle leader with their question and the circle leader could privately and randomly send out the questions to each circle member, making sure no one gets their own question. The questions could remain anonymous, although each person would know the question they're meditating on.

That's the best online option for this exercise. If you think of a better alternative, let me know!

The takeaway

This exercise doesn't necessarily turn into a mediumship message. You may connect with someone in Spirit or you may not and instead connect with your own intuition. Both are valid means for receiving useful, accurate information.

This exercise takes a lot of trust. You don't know what the question is and you don't even know who the message is for. But you trust what you get and you give it out in the safe, supportive environment of your development circle.

When I've done this exercise in my own circle, it's amazing to see not only how accurate people are with the information they get, but also how they often know who the message is for. They just have a sense. This has also been the case in the odd times someone has chosen their own question to answer.

Index card readings

This exercise is similar to the billet readings in the last exercise in that you write something down on pieces of paper—this time index cards—and pass them around and do a reading based on what you each get.

The difference is that these readings are of a person in Spirit and that you get to look at the name of the person.

How to do the exercise

You'll need enough index cards and pens for all the people in the circle.

- Each person writes down a name and/or relationship of someone in Spirit they personally know (no John Lennon or Elvis). You need the personal energetic connection to be able to tune into the person in Spirit accurately. Don't include your own name. Just write: "My grandmother, Yvette." Or "my grandmother" or "Yvette."

I've had circles where people write down the name of someone living who's going through a difficult situation or they're concerned about. You can do this, too, but then you're tapping into intuition, rather than mediumship, unless you connect with a relative in Spirit related to the person. It's your choice how you want to set the boundaries.

- The circle leader gathers the index cards, shuffles them and passes them out.

- It's OK for each person to look at the card they get and make sure it's not their own. If it is, shuffle again or switch with one or two circle members. Ideally, no one knows whose card they have or who has their card, but it's not imperative.

- Go into meditation for 8-10 minutes and tune in energetically with the person who's on the index card you're holding.

- Note your impressions and determine as much information as you can about the person in Spirit: name, age, appearance, gender, personality, occupation, habits, hobbies, etc.

- Some people like to take notes. I'm fine with my students taking notes, although some teachers aren't.

- After meditating on your index card for 8-10 minutes, go around the circle and share what you got. Each person reads what's written on their index card first, before sharing the message, so the person receiving the message knows it's for them. This can help with furthering the live connection to the person in Spirit as you're giving the message. It's OK if new information comes through as you're sharing.

Online

To do this exercise online, each person will need to message the circle leader the information they would have otherwise written on their index card.

The circle leader then sends a private message to each participant with the name/relationship for them to connect with, making sure everyone gets a different person than they wrote down (this is actually easier to do than when you're shuffling and handing out index cards).

You can then proceed as you would if you were meeting in person.

The takeaway

Being able to connect to specific people in Spirit is a skill that can be developed. I call it Dial-A-Spirit. This exercise helps you develop this ability. This means that, rather than being able to only bring through whoever shows up and is loudest during a reading, you can connect with the person or people your sitter really wants to hear from.

There are two schools of thought on this. One is that whoever shows up and that you connect with is who needs to be heard from. That may be true at times.

The other is that the people who come to you for a reading (if you're working professionally) will often have a specific person or people in mind who they want to connect with. If you can tune into them, you're providing a valuable service to your clients and the experience can be extremely healing.

Some mediums are easily able to Dial-A-Spirit. Some aren't. I believe it's an ability worth cultivating.

Hot potato readings

Hot potato readings are a great way to get people who are reluctant to share and give out messages to just go for it.

There's usually quite a lot of laughter involved when a circle does this exercise, because it involves a bit of physical activity and often a lot of dropping the ball. But Spirit loves laughter. It eases tension and helps everyone relax, while raising your vibration. So don't worry if this happens in your circle.

How to do the exercise

You'll need a soft ball that's easy to throw and catch, without damaging the room you're in or hurting the circle participants if they don't catch it.

- Choose one person to start as the sitter. The rest of the circle will focus on that person and give messages to them.

- Choose one person to start giving messages. This is often the circle leader. They hold the ball and give out a piece of information or message to the sitter.

- As soon as they've given their information, they pass the ball to another person in the circle.

- That person then immediately gives whatever information they get, then passes the ball to another person.

- Continue on through all the circle members, so that everyone has to blurt out something about the sitter.

- Then change sitters and do the exercise again, repeating with new sitters until everyone has been the sitter.

Online

Sadly, I don't know a way to play this online with an actual ball since the circle members will all be in separate physical locations.

However, it can be done. The circle leader can either start or call out the name of someone to start. Once that person has given their message, they choose who goes next, and so on.

The takeaway

This is a fun and powerful exercise. Part of developing mediumship is the ability to connect instantly with Spirit and receive messages. But we often don't trust what we get and feel we have to sit for a long time or strain and reach for it. This isn't true.

Trust what you get. Give what you get. That's what this exercise makes you do. It puts you on the spot and you can't get rid of the "hot potato" until you've given out some information.

The power of 3

First, a confession. There's no specific power of 3 that you magically invoke in this exercise that makes your mediumship easy and effortless.

However, asking for only 3 things, not the entirety of the answers in the universe, is manageable, right? The magic is in making it feel doable and not overwhelming.

How to do the exercise

There are 2 ways to do this exercise, either in pairs or as a circle as a whole.

In pairs

- Pair up with another person and sit across from each other.
- Both partners close their eyes and take a few deep breaths to settle themselves and calm their minds.
- Ask Spirit for 3 things about the other person that they need to know, right now, so they can travel the path of their highest good.
- Sit quietly for a few minutes and allow this information to come to you. Trust what you get.
- Share with each other what you got.
- Form new partners and repeat.

In a circle

- Go into a quiet meditation period.

General exercises – The power of 3

- During this time, each member of the circle focuses on the other members in turn, asking Spirit for 3 things they need to know, right now, to be on the path of their highest good.
- Notice what comes up. You can write brief notes if that's helpful.
- Once you get 3 things, express gratitude to Spirit and move on to the next person.
- After 10-15 minutes, the circle leader ends the meditation.
- Everyone shares what they got.

Online

This exercise doesn't translate well to being done online in pairs, unless you're able to easily switch partners in your breakout groups. To do it with all the members of the circle together, follow the instructions above.

The takeaway

You're only asking for 3 things. By being specific and realistic in your ask, it's easier for your brain to accept the information you get. We often put together lists of 3 as a normal part of our everyday language, so groupings of 3 things feel natural and good to you, which makes your brain happy and feels easier to do in mediumship work.

This is a good exercise for people who are still struggling to trust themselves and to feel brave enough to give out the information they get. When you do it as a partner exercise, it feels even safer, as there's only one other person hearing you and you feel less on-the-spot.

Claircognizance developing exercises

Claircognizance is "clear knowing" or direct knowledge from Spirit. It often feels like a thought has dropped into your head.

Information that comes through claircognizance is often linked to the other clairs and comes through as images, music, words or a gut feeling combined with a knowing of information, often about a person or situation.

One of the main qualities of information received through claircognizance is not knowing where the information came from or being able to make a logical train-of-thought connection to it from the thoughts you'd just been thinking prior. If it's information you suddenly know, then start to wonder where on Earth it came from, it's probably claircognizance.

It can often feel like information that your conscious mind observes, rather than information it creates. It also tends to lack emotional weight when it first comes in, and only becomes associated with emotion once you've had the chance to think about it a bit.

Ironically, this type of knowing is the one you often question the most, because it seems outlandish or bizarre and doesn't make sense that you would suddenly think it.

In terms of mediumship work, claircognizance can bring through information that may not come through in other ways. Because this knowledge is direct, it's information that you just know, without knowing where it came from. This knowledge could be related to any aspect of evidential information or the message itself.

Information through claircognizance comes in through your crown chakra, so ensuring this chakra at the crown of your head is clear and open will help in your development, as will the following exercises.

Inspired writing

Inspired writing, sometimes known as inspirational, impressional or automatic writing, comes through claircognizance.

There's a type of automatic writing that can be done as physical mediumship, but this exercise describes the mental mediumship variety, which I'll call inspired writing in an attempt not to be confusing. The difference between the two is the level of relaxation or trance you're in, as well as how aware you are of the information coming through.

With inspired writing, you're aware of the information that comes through, although it feels like it's coming from outside your conscious mind—either from your guides, another aspect of your higher self, or from someone in Spirit. With automatic writing, you're not usually aware of the information that's coming through, as you're in a trance state and Spirit is using your body to produce the writing.

Inspired writing is easier to begin practicing, and it gets easier with practice. The most important part is to set aside your critical thinking mind and take a step back. Allow whatever wants to come through to come through. It doesn't matter if it all seems like garbage at first. That's just part of the process.

How to do the exercise

You'll need either a pen and paper or a computer and keyboard. My preference is a computer keyboard, as I type quickly and the information flows through me more easily. But other people find more success with a pen and paper. Try both and see what works better for you.

Claircognizance exercises – Inspired writing

- You need to be in a relaxed meditative state for this exercise, so begin with a few minutes of mediation, while each person has their writing apparatus ready in front of them.
- When you feel ready to begin, write down or type whatever first comes to your mind. Literally whatever comes into your mind. First write one word. Then the next. Then the next.
- You can have your eyes closed or slightly open during this process. I prefer to have a soft gaze on the page if I'm handwriting, so I have a sense of where my pen is on the page. If I'm using a computer, I have a soft gaze on the keys, to ensure I'm hitting the right ones, without getting distracted by the words I'm writing.
- Don't focus on the words you're writing. Just allow them to come out, at whatever speed they come.
- It doesn't matter how long it takes between words. Just write the words as they come into your awareness.
- Remember that your conscious mind is only a spectator in this process, not a controller.
- Ignore spelling, punctuation and grammar.
- Continue writing for several minutes or until it feels like the information that's coming through is complete.
- After the exercise, each person can share what they received, if they want. Sometimes the information is deeply personal, and doesn't feel right to share in the moment. That's OK.

Online

This exercise is done the same way whether you're meeting in person or online.

Variations

The first few times you do this exercise, ask your Spirit guides and higher self to bring you information you need to know right now, for your highest good. It requires the least thinking on your part and allows you to relax into the trust needed to do this exercise successfully.

In later practices, try asking specific questions about yourself, your life and your path. I find it helpful to write the questions at the beginning of the session, allowing Spirit to answer them during the period of inspired writing.

You can also use this exercise to connect with a loved one in Spirit. You can communicate with your loved one in this way, by writing down your questions and waiting for the answers to come into your mind.

Troubleshooting

If the words that come through you seem like nonsense and don't make sense, it's OK. That's just your subconscious mind purging its junk and you'll eventually get to the good stuff. Keep going.

If it feels like it takes forever to get anything, or to get a second word after you get the first one, it's OK. Allow it the time it needs. If all you get is four words in a 15-minute session, that's totally fine. Don't go out searching for the words, just allow them to come into your awareness.

Claircognizance exercises – Inspired writing

Conversely, if too much information comes at you too quickly for you to understand and write or type, ask for it to slow down to a manageable rate.

The takeaway

This exercise allows you to tap into your own higher self and guides, and the knowledge and wisdom available there. It develops your trust with the process of stepping back and becoming an observer. It also teaches you to relax into a light state of trance.

Mediumship work can use several different levels of trance. Mental mediumship is the lightest, where you're mentally present and in control of your body, but somewhat removed. Inspired writing uses a fairly light state of trance—you're in control of your fingers writing, but not thinking about the words you're producing.

The trust needed to give messages this way is huge. You have to intrinsically trust your guides and higher self that the words that come out of your mouth will be of the highest good (and not, say, a stream of curse words, or whatever you worry may happen if you let go of the tight hold of control you have on yourself).

The voice that comes through in your inspired writing may sound like you, but a wiser, calmer, more knowing you. This is your inner voice, the bearer of your inner wisdom and knowledge. The more you connect with this voice, the stronger it gets. Over time, you'll be able to discern the difference between the information you receive through your own mind and its subconscious beliefs and information from Spirit and your higher self.

Define your symbols

Symbols and the information they bring can come through all of your intuitive or mediumistic senses, not just claircognizance. But, as they're closely connected to knowing, since the meaning of a symbol will often land in your mind with no explanation, I've put this exercise in the claircognizance section.

There are huge advantages for your mediumship work in developing your understanding of symbols. Essentially, working with symbols helps you become fluent in the language of Spirit. Like learning a new language, the more time you spend with symbols, the quicker you understand them and can begin using them in your life.

What I've also seen happen is that by intentionally working with specific symbols, you begin to get information through those familiar symbols more often. It helps makes your message work clearer and easier, using less energy to convey accurate information. It's like when two people speak different languages, but need to have a conversation. At first, they spend a lot of time mugging and miming, trying to get their point across. Once they have some language in common, while neither might be fluent, it's much easier to express what you need to say and to be understood. Working with symbols builds your vocabulary with Spirit, so that communication gets easier.

My teachers encouraged me to develop a symbol dictionary, with my own interpretations and understandings of the symbols I saw in my meditations and message work. I now encourage my students to create their own symbol dictionary, however it works for them. I created *The Symbol Dictionary*

Claircognizance exercises – Define your symbols

Workbook for that purpose, but you could also use a 3-ring binder with loose-leaf paper and A-Z dividers to keep it organized.

How to do the exercise

There are a couple of ways to do this exercise, either as a standalone exercise (option 1) or combined with other exercises in this book (option 2).

Option 1: Define your symbols

The circle leader will need a list of common symbols. You can find these in many books about psychic development, in *The Spiritual Symbols Workbook*, or you can compile a list of your own. There's a list of the symbols I often start with at the end of this explanation.

- The circle enters into a quiet meditation, eyes closed, with some slow breathing for a few minutes, to get centered and calm. The rest of the exercise is done with the eyes open.
- The circle leader reads one of the symbols on the list.
- Each person pauses in reflection for 20-30 seconds, perhaps closing their eyes or having a soft gaze, and writes down what comes up for them about that symbol.
- The circle leader reads the next symbol and you repeat the reflection and writing.
- Afterwards, go around the circle with each person briefly sharing a few words from each definition they wrote down. If another person's definition of what that symbol means rings true, individual circle members can add it to their own dictionary. If not, don't. Everyone will get their

Claircognizance exercises – Define your symbols

own understanding of what different symbols mean to them, which is why it's important to develop your own dictionary for yourself.

Here's a list of symbols to get you started:

- A star
- A rose
- A DNA helix
- Red wine
- Praying hands
- A cross
- A pyramid
- A butterfly
- Decay
- Chocolate
- An alpaca
- A blackbird
- A bear
- Pizza
- An attic
- A tea pot
- A compass
- A teddy bear
- A trampoline
- A toddler
- An oyster
- Peppermint
- A piggy bank
- A pin cushion
- Scrolls
- The number seven
- A parachute
- A peacock
- A bracelet
- Braided hair
- A carnation
- A cactus
- An airplane
- An altar
- An ear
- A coconut
- A graduation cap
- Smoke
- An umbrella
- A walnut

Claircognizance exercises – Define your symbols

- A watch
- A sunrise
- A worm
- A yin-yang symbol

Option 2: Define symbols as they come up

This isn't a separate exercise, but rather an add-on to any other exercise or meditation you do in your circle.

Keep your symbol workbook handy at all times, or have a piece of paper you can write down symbol meanings on and add to your personal symbol dictionary later.

During the sharing portion of each exercise, the circle leader notes the various symbols that come up in people's messages and impressions.

At the end of the exercise, for 5-10 minutes, the circle leader reads each symbol, one at a time with a pause between each, for reflection and sharing, similar to doing the exercise as a standalone exercise in option 1.

Online

Either option for this exercise is done the same way whether your circle meets in person or online.

The takeaway

While it sounds simple, there are several parts to this exercise as well as things at work as you're doing it.

The first is seeking your own understanding and meaning of a symbol. You can ask your inner self or your guides for the meaning for you, and then write it down.

The second is sharing what you got. This is helpful for you, but also for your other circle members. As you each hear

Claircognizance exercises – Define your symbols

another person's understanding of that symbol, you'll get intuitive feedback about the meaning of the symbol for you. Either you'll feel a pull, a sense of rightness or an upward shift in energy, which means this is also a correct interpretation for you. Or you'll feel a sinking energy or a feeling of retraction or discomfort, which means that it's not the correct meaning for you.

The third element is taking note of which of your intuitive senses come into play when you connect with each symbol. You'll likely get information about symbols from more than claircognizance. While this exercise is listed under ones to develop claircognizance, it's totally OK for you to see the symbol in your mind's eye or get energetic information in your body about it. You may also get a sound, scent or taste associated with it as well.

It's not really important which of your clairsenses you get information through, just notice it. It's more of an indicator of which of your intuitive senses are most active right now. Sometimes the ones you think you primarily use aren't actually your strongest intuitive senses, you just haven't quite realized it.

Clairvoyance developing exercises

Clairvoyance is also known as clear-seeing, clear-sight, intuitive sight or psychic sight. For some, the ability to see the future is an essential part of clairvoyance but, in mediumship, clairvoyance is more directly associated with the sense of sight and can occur in two different ways.

Some people literally see energy in physical form—as is the case where they see what we'd usually call a ghost as if it's a solid or semi-solid object. Or they may see lights, orbs or a coalescing of energy.

Others see images as if they are a memory of sight, like you do when you recall things you've seen before. For instance, if I say, "Imagine a cup of coffee." Do you picture a cup of coffee in your mind's eye? (You may also be able to smell it and taste it through the memory of smell and taste, but we'll get to those in later chapters.)

Sometimes these images are still, like a photograph, or come through as a short movie, an animated gif or a picture that moves, like the photos in the Harry Potter books. Your ability to picture something in your mind's eye is part of your ability to see clairvoyantly.

The connecting piece between these examples is the use of your psychic or intuitive sight—there's always an element of seeing.

Many people receive clairvoyant information in both of these ways—through their physical and intuitive eyes. And, even if you see energy as if it is coming through your physical eyes, you're still using your intuitive or third eye.

It doesn't really matter how you receive clairvoyant information—whether it's an image you see with what appears to be your physical eyes or with your mind's eye, like a memory of sight. You may see these images clearly and sharply, or they may seem somewhat fuzzy, vague or out-of-focus, like an old memory. You're also likely to use other psychic or intuitive senses along with clairvoyance, such as claircognizance, where you just know something you're seeing has a certain meaning or is from a certain era.

In terms of mediumship, clairvoyance allows you to see what someone in Spirit looks like, enabling you to describe them to the sitter to get confirmation and provide evidential information. It also lets you see symbols (although symbols can be associated with other clairsenses, they are most often visual) and other visual images that are part of the message.

The thing to do here, as always, is to trust yourself and don't second-guess your first impressions.

The following exercises will help you connect with and open your third eye and develop your clairvoyance.

Send and receive images

This exercise helps you develop your intuitive or psychic sight by focusing on visual images that you send and receive.

You'll need images of varied objects for this exercise. You can cut them out from magazines and paste them on pieces of paper (one image per page) or find them online and print them out. You can also use a card deck such as Melanie Barnum's *Psychic Symbols Oracle Cards* or a deck of Tarot cards. What you're looking for is a set of clear visuals of a variety of tangible things (rather than ideas, abstract concepts, or emotions), e.g. a ball of yarn, broccoli, a mug, a house, a phone, a pen. etc.

How to do the exercise

There are two ways to do this exercise: in pairs or in a circle format. Either way, the basic premise is the same. When it's each person's turn to go, they choose an image to focus on and send to the receiver.

The receiver(s) opens themselves to receiving the visual information and make note of whatever they get.

In pairs

- Break into pairs, sitting across from each other.
- Decide who'll be the sender first and who'll be the receiver.
- The sender chooses a card or image to focus on.
- Both people close their eyes and take a few cleansing breaths.

Clairvoyance exercises – Send and receive images

- The sender projects the visual image to the receiver by looking at the image and being in an open and accessible state. They don't need to try and send the image.
- The receiver notices the impressions they receive and writes them down (or makes a mental note to share later).
- After about a minute or two, at the most, the receiver shares what they got with the sender and the sender shares what the image was.
- The partners switch roles.
- After both partners have practiced sending and receiving, switch partners or each pick a new image.

In a circle

- Choose a member of the circle to start. They choose a random image from the card deck or your pages of images and keep it facing themselves so the other circle members can't see it.
- They should look at the image and be in a state of openness and pleasant expectation. They don't need to focus on beaming the image out.
- The rest of the circle members connect with the energy of the person holding the image and write down, or mentally note, their impressions.
- After a minute or two at the most, circle members go around the circle, sharing what they got.
- When all members have shared their impressions, the receiver shares the image they chose, showing it to everyone in the circle.

Clairvoyance exercises – Send and receive images

- The next person in the circle becomes the sender and this continues until each person in the circle has had a turn being the sender.

Online

- This is easiest to do in a group format, rather than dealing with the technology issues of using breakout rooms in your online space (but if you're comfortable with the technology and have enough people to have several partner groups, go for it).
- Each person in your online circle will need to have an image to focus on. Each member could use whatever deck of cards they have, or search for a specific image online and have the image up on their screen.
- Follow the rest of the instructions for the exercise, either done with partners or in the circle, with the receiver looking at the image they've chosen, and the receiver(s) noting what impressions they get.
- After a minute or two, the partner or circle members share what they got, and the sender shows the image, either by holding up the card or image to the webcam or sharing their screen with the image displayed.
- Switch to the next person in the circle.

Variations

When you work with clairvoyance, you most often are concentrating on the third eye, receiving information with your mind's eye.

For a variation on this exercise, try receiving information through your heart center instead. This taps more into your

Clairvoyance exercises – Send and receive images

clairsentience, but you may still sense images. Does this feel different?

The takeaway

Much like many of these exercises, one of the things you're learning is trust. Trust in yourself and the information you receive and trust in your fellow circle members to accept your sharing and support you.

You may find you get information in a variety of ways, not just visually. While this exercise is primarily about developing clairvoyance, information can also come through as thoughts, feelings, smells, colors or tastes. That's OK.

Take note of the way information about these visual symbols shows up for you and make a note of it in your journal or symbol workbook. The next time you receive information that's the same as what came through for each of the images in this exercise, make the connection and see if the meaning is the same as the image or symbol used in this exercise.

Something else to be aware of is that if you're using a tarot or psychic symbols card deck, there's often a lot of information on the cards beyond the main symbol. You may not get the main symbol exactly, but get the information in the background.

You'll also find that the images each person draws when it's their turn to be the sender will be relevant to their life, especially if you're using tarot or psychic symbols cards. So the information each person picks up, if it's not directly related to what's on the cards, may very well be related to the situation in the person's life that the symbol represents. When I've done this in my own development circle, that's always been the case.

Use photographs

This exercise enables you to begin getting and sharing mediumistic or intuitive information about real people. Use photos of people you know, so you can give feedback and confirmation. The people the photos are of can either be in Spirit or still alive in physical form.

If they are in Spirit, the information that comes through will usually be more mediumistic. If they're physically alive, it will be intuitive or psychic information. Neither of these is necessarily better or more desired than the other, in my opinion, it's just important to be able to distinguish the difference. It's totally normal for developing mediums to begin by getting psychic or intuitive information. When it comes down to it, it's all just energy and information.

How to do the exercise

This exercise is best done in a circle format (either in person or online), rather than in pairs. You'll need a photo from each participant of a loved one in their life.

- Each member of the circle brings a photograph, in an envelope (it doesn't need to be sealed, just enclosed in the envelope so you can't see it).
- There are two options for working with the photos:
    1. You can exchange photos randomly between members, with each person having someone else's photo.
    2. You can place one photo at a time in the center of the circle and all members focus on that one photo.

Clairvoyance exercises – Use photographs

- During the meditation, circle members tune into the photo and make either mental or written notes of the impressions they get.

- If you're using one photo for all members, have a shorter meditation so you can switch photos and do it again. If each person has a photo to focus on, have a longer meditation.

- At the end of the meditation, each circle member shares what they received.

- When everyone has had a chance to share, take the photo out of the envelope and allow the person who brought it to share what they know about the person in the photo to confirm the information received.

Online

If you're working online, each person should send a photo—either digitally or a hard copy via postal mail—to the circle leader.

Everyone in the circle will tune into the same photograph during the exercise.

- During the meditation, the circle leader either puts a hardcopy of the photograph, in an envelope, in view of the webcam, or displays a digital photo on their screen, without sharing the screen with the rest of the circle.

- The other circle members tune into the photo and make notes of their impressions.

- After a few minutes, each circle member shares what they received.

- The circle leader then either takes the printed photo out of the envelope and shows it to the group or they share their screen showing the digital photo. The person who the photo belongs to can then share information to confirm the impressions and messages received about it.
- The circle leader then switches to a new photo and you repeat the process.

A note on taking notes: When beginning to develop your abilities, it's fine to write down what you're getting so you remember it later and feel more confident sharing it. Eventually, you'll want to get to a place where you're doing it live without notes, but for right now you're practicing, so don't worry about it. Take notes if you find it helpful.

The takeaway

By not looking at the photographs before sharing the information you get about them, you're really building your trust with yourself and your abilities. Remember that what you get at this point doesn't matter as much as the process of doing the work of development.

It's extremely likely you'll get some accurate information about the person in the photo.

Notice how the information comes through for you. While this is a clairvoyance developing exercise—because the object is physical and visual—you'll also get information through other senses. Make note of that.

Sense each other's color

Color is a vibrant form of energy that's around us all the time. We're often attracted to certain colors and may have strong feelings of dislike or aversion for other colors.

The power of this exercise is in its simplicity. You're not looking for anything more complicated than sensing another person's color.

This is similar to, although not the same as, seeing aura colors.

How to do the exercise

This is a guided exercise that the circle leader should lead the others through.

- Guide the circle members into a quiet, meditative state, with the intention of opening up and developing your intuitive sight.
- Then lead the circle through these steps:
  - Bring your conscious awareness inside your own body.
  - Take a few breaths here, settling your energy and grounding yourself.
  - Focus your awareness on another person in the circle.
  - Imagine your intuitive sight seeing them as energy.
  - What color predominantly comes up?
  - Don't overthink it. Just trust it and note it.

- Relax your focus and bring your awareness back inside your own body.
- Take a cleansing breath and move on to the next person in the circle.
- Continue this process for each person.
- Afterward, share your impressions.

Online

Follow the above directions.

The takeaway

They key components of this exercise are trusting what color you get for each person and then sharing that information.

When I've led this exercise in my own home circle, it's amazing how many people get the same colors for the same people.

This is a great exercise for developing your trust in yourself and receiving confirmation about what you get.

Read auras

Some people who are clairvoyant see auras easily and clearly with their intuitive sight and use this information as part of their readings and message work.

The dictionary definition of an aura is "the distinctive atmosphere or quality that seems to surround and be generated by a person, thing, or place."

In terms of mediumship and psychic development, an aura is the band of energy that surrounds all living things. This is often seen as color and is basically made up of specific frequencies of vibrations that can provide information about the health and energetic makeup of that person or object.

Sometimes people also see successive bands of energy further away, which may be related to our different energy bodies—etheric, emotional, mental, astral, celestial, etc.

There are several elements to be aware of in auras, in terms of understanding the meaning of what you're seeing or sensing.

Color and clarity

What are the colors of the aura? Are they bright and vibrant or dull? How clear are the colors?

Location and shape

Where do you see certain colors in the aura? Colors, and their corresponding clarity and vibrancy, may relate either to the adjacent physical areas or to the chakras associated with those body parts, e.g. third-eye chakra around the head, root chakra around the pelvis and hips.

Consistency and spikes

Is the energy or color spiky or smooth? This is an indication to the overall health of the corresponding areas of the body.

How to do the exercise

You'll need a plain background, preferably white, although a light color can work as well. The easiest way to accomplish this is to hang up a sheet and put a chair in front of it so each circle member can take turns sitting in front of it.

- Choose a sitter to go first and have them sit in the chair in front of the sheet or plain background.

- The rest of the circle focuses on reading their aura.

- Look either at the sitter's third eye or to the side of their body, perhaps just to the side of their head or shoulder. Relax your eyes and keep your focus on that spot for about a minute.

- While continuing to look at the same spot, relax your eyes and allow them to pick up information in your peripheral vision.

- Their aura may begin to appear as lines of wavy energy—like heat radiating off a road in the summer—or as an impression of color. You don't necessarily need to see the color. It may come through as a sense of a color. It may feel yellow, for instance, without it being a bright yellow color.

- You may also get more of a sense of energy, rather than a distinct color impression.

- Usually, the background right around the person is brighter or different color than the background further away from them.

- Once the circle has had a few minutes to read the first sitter's aura, share your impressions around the circle.

- Switch sitters and repeat, going around the circle until each member has had their aura read.

Online

You can do this is in a similar way to an in-person circle, by taking turns and having everyone else in the circle focus on reading the aura of each of the members in turn.

You'll need to highlight the video feed of the person who's turn it is to have their aura read, so that they appear as the main video on the screen. Each member will also need to find a good place in their house, with a plain background, to sit in front of. It's a little trickier to do it online, but it can certainly be done.

The takeaway

This is a fun, uplifting exercise for a development circle and a refreshing change from the usual exercises. My students always enjoy exploring their intuitive sight with this exercise.

What do aura colors mean?

Aura colors aren't quite as simple as red means anger, yellow means strength, etc. Red, for instance, can also mean independence, or it can indicate inflammation of the body area it appears near.

You can approach this in a couple of different ways. You can learn about the typical symbolism of different colors, or you can use your intuition to discern what different colors mean (and maybe even write your definitions down in your symbol dictionary).

Also remember that color isn't the only thing to look for when reading an aura. Clarity, location and consistency also give useful information.

In general, the clearer, brighter and more vibrant an aura is, the better the person (or plant or pet) is doing. A vibrant aura indicates clear energy, without a lot of junk (e.g., negative thoughts, limiting beliefs, subconscious blocks, damaging habits or behaviors).

A uniform aura indicates a healthy and balanced body, whereas areas of spikes or holes show where there may be physical discomfort or disease.

Aura or afterimage?

If you look at anything for long enough, when you look away or close your eyes, you'll see an afterimage. But an aura isn't the same as an afterimage.

An afterimage has precisely the same shape as original images. But an afterimage of an object surrounded by its aura is larger than the original image. You can see both a person's afterimage and their aura for a few seconds when you close your eyes after looking at them.

Also note that afterimages do not have any color to them. Auras often do.

Strengthen and focus your third eye

This exercise gives your third eye an energetic workout, which will help to strengthen it and build your endurance in using it. It also increases your connection with your intuitive sight and develops your ability to see symbols clearly.

How to do the exercise

- Have one person lead the group, as it makes it easier for everyone to relax into the exercise and maintain their focus.
- As you sit in meditation, focus your awareness on your third eye, just above and between your eyebrows.
- Visualize the number 1 in your mind's eye.
- See it clearly. What color is it? How large is it? Is it a flat 2D image or 3D?
- Manipulate how it appears: Ask the number to grow bigger in size, to come closer, to change color, to change font, etc.
- Stay with this number for 20-30 seconds, then move onto another number.
- Continue this process for 3-5 minutes or however long the group can endure, with the leader calling out any number they want. (You can also proceed incrementally, 1, 2, 3., etc., but random numbers may keep things interesting and help everyone stay focused).

Don't strain yourself during this exercise—start out with a short time duration until you build your intuitive eye muscles!

Variations:

- Letters of the alphabet
- Colors
- Common symbols

Online

You do this exercise the same way whether your circle meets in person or online.

The takeaway

This exercise helps sharpen and strengthen your intuitive sight. You learn how to see symbols and images clearly and how to manipulate them so you can see them better. This is an important skill in mediumship work as fuzzy and indistinct information isn't particularly useful.

Plus, it strengthens your connection with your third eye and your mind's eye.

Clairaudience developing exercises

Clairaudience, or clear hearing, is the ability to hear messages and information from Spirit in the form of music, sounds or voices.

Clairaudient information is heard with your physical and intuitive ears.

Sounds can be heard both as what seems like the memory of hearing or as external audible noises. Sometimes sounds come across as an inner voice in your head, like recalling the memory of a sound you've heard before, or externally, like a snatch of music on the breeze, someone calling your name, or hearing knocking in the room around you.

Another way you get clairaudient information is when you hear a song on the radio and you know, somewhere within yourself, that it's a message for you from Spirit or from a loved one in Spirit. This combines clairaudience with clairsentience: your physical ears hear the song that everybody else can hear, but your inner knowing understands that you are hearing it at that time specifically and especially for you.

In your mediumship work, clairaudience can bring evidential information in a variety of ways: hearing the person in Spirit's name, hearing a favorite song, or hearing words or phrases they used to say, as just a few examples.

The following exercises will help you develop clairaudience by opening, clearing and strengthening your throat chakra (the

Clairaudience developing exercises

center for communication) and developing your ability to tune into specific sounds.

Follow the instrument

This exercise helps you to learn how to tune into a specific frequency, which will help you to receive messages more loudly and clearly. You do this by following one instrument throughout a piece of music.

How to do the exercise

This is a simple exercise and is done the same way whether you're meeting in person or online. Choose a piece of music to play. Classical music works well, but any style can work. Don't overthink it. Just pick a song you like to start with and then try it with several different songs.

- With the circle ready and relaxed, eyes closed, start the song.
- Each person picks out one instrument in the tune and follows it through the piece. Stay with it as it comes and goes, getting quieter and louder, throughout the song.
- Share your experiences after. What instrument did you choose? Were you able to stay with it?

Online

If you're meeting online, make sure everyone can hear the music that the circle leader plays. You may want to experiment with playing it from your computer speakers, sharing the audio with the other participants, and playing it from an external device, such as your phone, an MP3 player with a speaker, or a CD player.

The takeaway

This is often a surprisingly difficult exercise at first. Unless you're a trained musician, this can be harder than it seems. However, with practice it will become easier.

You're training your ears to focus on certain sounds and frequencies, bringing them to the forefront of your attention, even when they are tuned into a sound that's not the most prevalent part of the music.

This is an important skill to learn so that, when you receive messages from Spirit but they aren't coming through as loudly or clearly as you'd like, you can focus on what you want to hear and not be distracted by other information that may also be coming through or be in your external environment.

Listen to the sounds around you

This exercise involves simply listening to the sounds that are already present in your physical environment. It doesn't seem particularly mystical, but it helps you become more aware of the information you pick up with your ears.

How to do the exercise

You'll focus your hearing on 3 different locations during the exercise, each for 2-3 minutes: near, far and within. You can extend the amount of time you spend focused on each location for as long as is comfortable for your circle participants.

This exercise is best led by the circle leader.

- Guide the circle into a relaxed, meditative state. Then use the following script to guide the circle through the exercise.
- First, focus on the sounds in the room around you.
  - What sounds do you hear close to you?
  - Can you name them?
  - Where do they originate from?
- Next, extend your hearing.
  - What do you hear beyond your immediate surroundings?
  - How far can you stretch your ears?
  - Where are the sounds coming from?
- Then, bring your hearing so close to you that go you within your body and hear its messages to you.

Clairaudience exercises – Listen to the sounds around you

- Can you hear your breath?
- Can you hear your heart beating?
- Can you hear your cells moving around?
- Does your body have a message for you to hear?
* Bring your awareness back up out of your body into the room around you.
* Feel the weight of your body in the chair, your feet on the floor, your hands in your lap. Wiggle your fingers and toes and gently open your eyes.
* Share your experiences. What did you each hear?

Online

This exercise is done the same way, whether your circle meets in person or online. If you're meeting online, as you're each in a different location, you'll hear different sounds.

The takeaway

How does becoming aware of the sounds around you help you hear people in Spirit? It doesn't, directly. But it does help you distinguish between what's in your physical environment and what's coming in energetically from Spirit.

Developing your physical senses and becoming more aware of them and how to use them also helps you develop the corresponding intuitive or mediumistic sense.

Being more connected to your physical body helps you in your mediumship, as your physical self is the instrumentality you use to connect with Spirit, receive and understand messages.

Clairaudience exercises – Listen to the sounds around you

This exercise also allows you to get quiet and to be in the moment. We often don't really hear the sounds around us, or have learned to tune them out. Spirit speaks in the quiet moments. You want to be able to tune into the still small voice within you.

Imagine sounds

This exercise strengthens your intuitive hearing muscles, allowing them to hear sounds from Spirit more easily.

This is a similar exercise to the clairvoyance developing exercise where you visualize numbers, letters and objects. When you work on clairaudience, you allow the sound of different things to come into your consciousness.

How to do the exercise

You'll need a leader to read the list of sounds.

- Bring the circle into a quiet, calm place, breathing evenly with eyes closed.
- The circle leader reads a list of everyday sounds, pausing in between each sound. A suggested list is below the instructions. Feel free to add your own.
- Guide the circle to imagine the sound, hear the memory of the sound within yourself.
- Ask the circle members:
  - What impressions do you get?
  - What comes up?
- Everyone can jot their impressions down on paper, or make a mental note.
- The circle leader continues through the list for 5-10 minutes.
- Afterwards, share your experiences.

Clairaudience exercises – Imagine sounds

This exercise is a great one to combine with developing your symbol dictionary. :)

Online

This exercise follows the same format, whether your circle meets in person or online.

Suggested sounds:

- A car
- A piano
- A baby laughing
- Your favorite song
- Your mother's voice
- A jackhammer
- A bell ringing
- A door slamming
- Birds singing
- A baby crying
- A siren
- Someone saying, "Yes!"
- Computer keys being typed
- Footsteps
- A dog barking
- The garbage truck
- A judge's gavel

Clairaudience exercises – Imagine sounds

- A hammer hitting a nail
- Ice cubes in a glass
- A broom sweeping
- Wind chimes in the breeze

The list could go on and on. What sounds do you hear in your everyday life? Think of those and imagine them.

The takeaway

This is a fun exercise because you learn what you associate with certain sounds. And you learn what's the same or different for others. It can help you develop your symbol dictionary and it flexes your memory-of-sound muscles.

Plus, it engages your imagination. Developing mediums are often afraid of their imagination when it comes to connecting with Spirit. Rather than a way of connecting, imagination becomes a reason to doubt. "What if I'm just imagining it?"

Imagination is good. It comes from Spirit and it's part of your connection to Spirit. Your imagination is one of the ways that Spirit communicates with you. So listen to it—literally, in this case—and believe in it.

You may find that, as you imagine these sounds, your other senses go to work, too—especially your sense of smell. That's because your senses of smell and taste are also linked to your throat chakra. So when you invoke your intuitive ears and work on clairaudience, you're also opening up your intuitive sense of taste (clairgustance) and smell (clairalience).

Information may also come in through seeing and feeling (both touch and emotion). For example, when you think of the sound of your mother's voice, an emotion is very likely to come

Clairaudience exercises – Imagine sounds

up with that—whether it's a warm loving feeling, a longing for something lost, or a feeling of dread and revulsion, depending on the relationship you had with your mom. You may also get a whiff of your mother's scent, or the memory of it, and see her in your mind's eye. This is totally normal.

Tune into Spirit FM

This exercise helps you tune into information from Spirit, focusing on clairaudience.

It's vital, as you develop your abilities, to learn how to control them—whether that's turning them on and off, or turning the volume up or down.

In this exercise, you'll imagine your clairaudience ability as if it's a radio receiver, able to pick up and tune into different frequencies on the Spirit band (a bit like AM or FM radio, but for Spirit communication). That's what clairaudient information is—an energy frequency that you can tune into. I call this Spirit FM.

How to do the exercise

This is a quiet exercise, almost a meditation. The circle leader should guide everyone into meditation, clearing the mind and the initial tuning in to Spirit FM, and back out again at the end of the exercise. During the exercise itself, each person tunes in independently.

- Guide the circle into a quiet, meditative state.
- Guide the circle to clear their mind by letting go of all the things that came before this moment, imagining their thoughts as birds, flying away and leaving a clear blue sky.
- Imagine there's a tuning knob on the side of your head, that you can use to scan up and down the frequency band of Spirit communication, until you find a frequency that's broadcasting a signal.

Clairaudience exercises – Tune into Spirit FM

- If you begin to hear something, slow down your scanning and listen.
- If it's indistinct or not quite understandable, fine tune the frequency.
- If it's too loud or too soft, adjust the volume.
- Once you've tuned into this frequency for a few minutes, try another station.
- At the end of the exercise, make sure you turn off your psychic radio.
- Share in the circle what you each experienced.

Online

You do this exercise the same way whether you're meeting in person or online.

The takeaway

Tuning into an audible communication from Spirit is similar to sitting in a cafe or other place with people having conversations, and tuning into one of the voices to pick up the conversation and words being said. You may also get the feeling behind the words, or the emotional state of the person speaking, or being spoken to. Practicing tuning into these kinds of conversations will actually help you develop the skill of doing it clairaudiently. It's not eavesdropping, it's psychic development!

You may or may not get a lot of information in this exercise. Think of it as an experiment, a "try and it see what happens" experience. As long as you're setting your intention for the highest good, you're protected and safe.

It also teaches you to control this ability, not only by tuning in to different frequencies, but by intentionally turning it on and off. You don't want to walk around all day with your intuitive ears open to Spirit, which means you need to practice activating and deactivating your awareness.

Clairgustance developing exercises

Clairgustance, or clear tasting, is your intuitive sense of taste. You really can get energetic information from Spirit through your taste buds.

What tastes can you pick up on energetically? Pretty much anything you can taste with your physical tongue and taste buds. Intuitive tasting experiences can be bitter, sweet, salty, sour or umami. The taste is usually experienced just as if you had that substance in your mouth or as a memory of taste.

Often, clairgustance experiences are accompanied by your other intuitive senses, especially clairalience (clear smelling). For example, the smell and taste of baked goods are so closely related it's hard to distinguish between them.

You can get some really useful information for message work through clairgustance. The taste of a favorite food of the person in Spirit, for instance, can provide valuable, evidential information.

Clairgustance information can also provide clues as to how someone died—a bitter chemical taste from drugs or poison, the iron-rich tang of blood, or the acrid bile of vomit can all provide evidential information.

This clairsense is connected to your throat chakra.

Developing clairgustance doesn't lend itself to many group exercises. In general, developing your sense of taste, eating mindfully, being aware of what you eat, and expanding your

Clairgustance developing exercises

taste horizons will help you develop clairgustance. However, it can be developed using the following exercises.

Develop your intuitive sense of taste

This exercise involves tasting a variety of flavors together, in a mindful, meditative way, in order to get information about the different foods and tastes.

How to do the exercise

Gather a sampling of foods and beverages. A suggested list is below the instructions.

Cut them into bite-sized portions and put them onto separate plates that can be passed around for each person to take a piece. Give each person in the circle their own cup that you can pour beverages into (rather than passing around a mug that everyone shares).

- Gather the food items with differing tastes.
- The circle leader guides everyone into a meditative state.
- Pass around the plate or beaker of liquid so each person can take a portion.
- Each person takes one item at a time and has a sip or a bite.
- Hold the substance in your mouth. Allow your taste buds to fully taste it, absorbing and experiencing its flavor.
- What thoughts come into your awareness?
- What memories does the taste connect with?
- What feelings come up?
- What knowledge, inner knowing or information do you associate with the food or drink?

Clairgustance exercises –Your intuitive sense of taste

- Write this down in your symbol dictionary workbook or journal.
- Continue through the exercise to the next food or drink, perhaps having a sip of water in between to clear your palate.
- After you've gone through all the foods/drinks, share what you got.

Suggested foods/beverages (feel free to add your own and substitute as needed for food sensitivities):

- Water
- Cheeses (swiss, cheddar, mozzarella)
- Processed meats (ham, turkey, bologna)
- Fruits (strawberry, banana, orange, etc.)
- Black coffee
- Chocolate
- Sour candy
- Green tea

A variation

You could gather the list of foods and put them in separate, numbered containers, and essentially feed them, one at a time, to each circle member while their eyes are closed.

This can help develop your sense of taste by learning to discern which food is which and what each tastes like.

A couple of caveats about doing the exercise this way: there's no online option and you must ensure that no one in the circle has any food sensitivities to any of the foods or drinks you're using. That said, it's a fun way to try the exercise!

Online

This exercise is trickier to do online, but can be done. The circle as a whole needs to agree on which foods and drinks to get together and each person is responsible for getting them for themselves. You can then follow the directions above.

The takeaway

When you allow yourself to pay attention, the food you eat will give you information. It'll bring up memories, evoke feelings, and your body will even tell you if it's a good idea for you to be eating it or not. Because you're quiet and listening for signals, you're much more likely to get this information.

It also helps to develop your overall sense of taste and build your taste dictionary. Tastes from Spirit are most likely going to come through as things you've already experienced. Taking the time to really taste gives you more accurate data to get good information from Spirit.

Imagine tastes

A way to develop clairgustance without eating or drinking any actual substances is to engage your imagination and the memory of taste.

Rather than assembling a bevy of tastes to put in your mouth, in this exercise you'll use images of various foods.

This makes it easier for everyone to participate, no matter their location, dietary restrictions or food preferences.

How to do the exercise

Find images of foods and drinks with strong, distinct or familiar flavors. Either cut them out of magazines, or look for them online and print them out or, if your circle meets online, save them into an electronic document. If you're not able to get images of these foods, you can also just read the list aloud.

- The circle leader guides the circle into a quiet, meditative state.
- Allow your conscious awareness to move within.
- Guide the circle members to visualize their throat chakra opening up and being cleared of any energy that doesn't serve the highest good.
- The circle leader reads the name of each item and/or shows its picture to the rest of the circle.
- Each person looks at the item and allows themself to experience its taste.
- The circle leader asks:
  - What comes up as you look at the image?

Clairgustance exercises – Imagine tastes

- Can you taste it? Can you feel it in your mouth?
- What does your intuition tell you about it?
- Each person makes notes in their symbol dictionary or journal.
- Once you've gone through all the items, share your impressions.

Online

The circle leader can share their screen to show the images they've saved in an electronic document (such as Google docs or Word), moving through each image in turn, and/or reading its name aloud.

Ideas for foods (feel free to add your own as you're inspired):

- Pizza
- Ham
- Blue cheese
- Strawberries dipped in chocolate
- Coffee beans
- Apple sauce
- Hot sauce
- Nori seaweed sheets
- Roasted chickpeas
- Potato chips
- Vanilla cake
- Spaghetti

Clairgustance exercises – Imagine tastes

- Heavy whipping cream
- Soy sauce
- Green peas
- Sharp cheddar

The takeaway

It's likely you'll get impressions through your other senses, beyond your sense of taste. You might get a smell, or a sensation in your body about the food or drink. You might get a connection to a loved one in Spirit, or some other information.

Some people like to combine clairgustance and clairalience exercises together, so you could potentially combine this with the Imagine Smells exercise in the next section.

Ask for tastes from Spirit

Rather than using actual food, images or food, or suggestions of food, you can ask Spirit for a memory of taste. You do this by connecting in with a loved one in Spirit and asking for their communication to come through in the form of a taste.

It may sound a little odd, but if you've got any folks in Spirit who liked to eat good food or to cook, they'll be delighted to play along.

How to do the exercise

This exercise can be done in pairs or with the whole circle. Each person will bring to mind and heart a loved one in Spirit to ask their partner or the rest of the circle to receive a taste from.

In a circle

- Taking turns, one person names a loved one in Spirit for the rest of the circle to meditate on and connect with.
- Everyone closes their eyes and gets into a meditative state.
- Each person asks the person in Spirit to give them a taste. You can say their name, or relationship to the sitter, in your mind to call to them. The sitter can do this as well.
- Stay in meditation for about 2 minutes, noticing the sensations you feel in your mouth and throat.
- Open your eyes and share your impressions around the circle.
- Switch to the next person in the circle.

In pairs

- Split up into pairs.
- Each person in the pair shares the name of a loved one in Spirit—either at the same time or taking turns
- Follow the directions above for the circle.
- Share your impressions.
- Switch partners until each person has partnered with everyone else in the circle.

Online

- If you want to do this in pairs, you'll need to use breakout spaces, which might get a bit tricky when you switch partners.
- To do this as a circle, follow the instructions above for the circle

The takeaway

Many of us love food and certainly have favorite foods and flavors, and meals we like to make. The same is true for your friends and loved ones in Spirit. Sharing a flavor or taste is an interesting and fairly easy way to make a connection and send information as it can be specific and unexpected.

These kind of impressions—tastes (and smells) from Spirit—can be useful, evidential information. Including your intuitive sense of taste gives you more information to work with and convey, making your message work more reliable and meaningful. This exercise gives you an opportunity to open up your sense of taste and get a sense of what it feels like to receive information in this way.

Clairalience developing exercises

Clairalience, or clear smelling, is your intuitive or psychic sense of smell. It's also known as clairolfaction or clairessence.

Like your intuitive sense of taste, your intuitive sense of smell is an often-ignored sense. That's a shame, as it can be very clear and powerful. The two are actually related, just like your physical senses of smell and taste usually work together.

Clairalience is connected to your memory and carries with it a powerful emotional component, linking it to clairsentience (clear feeling).

Your senses of smell and taste are primal senses, strongly related to your survival instinct. Like clairaudience and clairgustance, clairalience is connected to your fifth chakra at your throat. It's also connected to your root chakra at the base of your spine.

As with any other intuitive sense, clairalience can give you information about a loved one in Spirit, insight into your health or knowledge of your path in life. In terms of loved ones in Spirit, you may smell their perfume or another smell associated with them—such as cigarette smoke, engine grease or cinnamon rolls—and immediately sense a connection to them.

This can be useful in providing evidential information about someone when you're doing a reading. I'll often know that a person in Spirit was a smoker because I get a whiff of smoke where I didn't smell any on my client when they arrived. Just like all the other intuitive senses, clairalience can also occur in

Clairalience developing exercises

conjunction with other intuitive senses—such as seeing an older woman who feels like a doting grandma and smelling baked goods while also getting the taste of the yummy goodies in your mouth.

Smells can also come in as a means of communicating a message, such as smelling baby poop when the sitter is pregnant, or about to be, and they don't yet know it.

Clairalience can be experienced as the memory of smell or as a distinct, physical scent that others may or may not be able to smell as well.

You can also experience clairalience as energy that either smells right or wrong somehow. Ever heard the phrases, "Something smells off here" or "I smell a rat"? Through clairalience, you can smell where energy is blocked or the body is experiencing disease.

The following exercises will help you develop your clairalience.

Smell each other's energy

Smelling each other's energy may sound like an odd exercise. But it's really not that strange! You're tapping into the energy frequency of smell around each of the other participants.

How to do the exercise

You can do this exercise in a group or in pairs. The circle leader can lead the exercise through the first cycle of connecting with a sense of smell and then the circle members can individually take it from there.

- Sitting in a circle, or across from your partner, go into a meditative state with the intention of opening up and developing your intuitive sense of smell.

- First, bring your conscious awareness inside yourself and settle your energy.

- Then, allow your conscious awareness to extend out to another person in the circle, or to your partner. Imagine yourself breathing in the energy around them.

- As you breathe in their energy, ask to receive smell impressions.

- What do you smell and connect with? If you also receive information in the form of taste, sounds or images or colors, that's OK. If so, what does that color smell like? What does the taste smell like?

- Record your impressions, then withdraw your conscious awareness from their energy field and allow yourself a deep cleansing breath.

- Move on to the next person in the circle or switch partners.
- Share your impressions.

Online

If you're meeting online, do the exercise with the whole circle and follow the directions above.

The takeaway

This exercise works to open up your intuitive sense of smell. Your sense of smell is a strong and important one, but it's generally considered rude to go around physically sniffing other people.

This is a way of connecting with your intuitive smelling ability, in a way that's non-obtrusive.

As you'll have learned from your own experience and the sharing of your circle members, it can give you interesting information.

When I've done this exercise in my development circle, several people in the circle will get the same smells, colors and impressions for a particular person. This underrated intuitive sense can really be remarkable.

Imagine smells

This exercise helps you strengthen your physical sense of smell to heighten your intuitive smell. Visualizing sights, sounds, tastes and smells strengthens their related intuitive senses.

How to do the exercise

Look online or in magazines for images of different items with strong scents. A suggested list is below the instructions. Cut them out, print them out or save them into an electronic document.

If you're not able to find these images easily, you can also read the list, one by one, during the exercise. Being able to see the images, though, makes it easier to connect to their associated scent.

This exercise is best led by the circle leader throughout.

- Guide the circle get into a calm, relaxed, meditative state.
- Allow conscious awareness to move within.
- Read the name of each item and show its picture to the circle.
- Each person looks at the item and allows themself to experience its smell.
- Ask the circle:
- What comes up as you look at the image?
- What does your intuition tell you about it?

Clairalience exercises – Imagine smells

- Each person makes notes in their symbol dictionary or journal.
- Once you've gone through all the items, share your impressions.

Online

To do this exercise online, save the images into an electronic document and have the circle leader share their screen, while scrolling through each image and saying its name.

Ideas for images:

- Pizza
- Oranges
- Lavender
- Garbage
- Baby diapers
- Tobacco smoke
- Wood smoke
- Lilac flowers
- Mint
- Oregano
- Thyme
- Rosemary
- Lemons
- Bananas
- Pine needles

Clairalience exercises – Imagine smells

- A bottle of perfume
- Chocolate
- Coffee
- Dirt
- Vanilla
- Garlic
- Onions
- Vinegar
- Rose petals
- Pencil shavings
- Ginger

The takeaway

You'll likely notice how quickly you connect to the memory of smell with each of these items. You may also get a flash of an image associated with that smell, perhaps the herb growing in your own garden, a childhood memory, or a loved one in Spirit.

Your sense of smell is strongly linked to your emotions and memories and it can be a powerful way of receiving information from Spirit.

Strengthen your sense of smell

This exercise is concrete way to connect with your sense of smell. Unfortunately, it only works for an in-person circle. But, if you're up for it, it's a great way to strengthen your sense of smell.

How to do the exercise

Using the list of smells below, assemble as many of the items as you can in lidded containers. Number the containers but make sure you can't see what's inside. An alternative to using various foods and herbs is to use bottles of essential oils with the labels covered and numbered.

This exercise is best led by the circle leader.

- Guide the circle members into a quiet, meditative state.
- Pass each container around the circle one at a time, letting the circle members know what number the container is.
- With their eyes closed, each person opens the container and smells its contents.
- Ask the circle members:
  - What is the smell?
  - What comes up as you connect with the smell?
  - What other senses are being activated?
- Each person writes down their impressions.
- After you've gone through all the containers, the circle leader can disclose what was in each container.

- Share your impressions—not just if you got them right, but what else came up during the exercise.

Online

There's no way I've thought of to do this for an online circle, that's not incredibly time consuming with each person gathering each of the scents. In that case, each person would know what's in each container, which loses some benefits of the exercise.

Ideas for smells:

- Oranges
- Lavender
- Tobacco or a cigarette
- Charcoal
- Lilac or other strongly scented flowers
- Mint
- Oregano
- Thyme
- Rosemary
- Lemons
- Bananas
- Pine needles
- Perfume
- Dark chocolate
- Coffee

Clairalience exercises – Strengthen your sense of smell

- Dirt
- Vanilla
- Garlic
- Onions
- Vinegar
- Rose petals
- Pencil shavings
- Ginger

The takeaway

Because you can't see what's in each container, this exercise helps build trust and confidence. You've got to trust your nose and intuition to determine what each smell is.

It also helps you build your smell database, so that you can more accurately understand the smell impressions you get from Spirit.

Ask for smells from Spirit

This exercise is similar to the clairgustance exercise asking for tastes from Spirit. You follow the same format (which I'll repeat below), but ask for a smell, rather than a taste.

How to do the exercise

This exercise can be done in pairs or with the whole circle. Each person will bring to mind and heart a loved one in Spirit to ask their partner or the rest of the circle to receive a smell from.

In a circle

- Taking turns, each person names a loved one in Spirit for the rest of the circle to meditate on and connect with.
- Close your eyes. Get into a meditative state.
- Clear your throat chakra. Imagine sapphire blue light filling your throat, nose, mouth and ears, clearing away anything that's not serving you.
- Ask the named person in Spirit to give you a smell.
- Stay in meditation for 2-3 minutes, noticing the sensations you sense through your sense of smell.
- Share your impressions.
- Switch to the next person in the circle.

In pairs

- Split up into pairs.
- Each person in the pair shares the name of a loved one in Spirit—either at the same time or taking turns.

Clairalience exercises – Ask for smells from Spirit

- Follow the directions above for working in a circle.
- Share your impressions.
- Switch partners until each person has partnered with everyone else in the circle.

Online

- If you want to do this in pairs, you'll need to use breakout spaces, which might get a bit tricky when you switch partners.
- To do this as a circle, follow the "in a circle" instructions above.

The takeaway

The learning from this exercise is similar to asking for smells from Spirit. You're able to experience what a smell from Spirit is actually like, by asking for information through this sense.

It's vital to trust what you get, especially because this is a sense you may not be used to using to receive information from Spirit. The smells you get may surprise you. They may even seem embarrassing. Share them anyway.

Notice especially what smells you get at first, right after you ask for them. Those initial impressions are often the most accurate, before you go searching for information, trying to interpret it or second-guessing yourself.

Clairsentience developing exercises

Clairsentience is intuitive or psychic feeling and is closely connected to what we usually think of as intuition. It's based on the ability to tune into the energetic vibrations of people, objects and places and to interpret those vibrations into meaning.

There are two aspects to clairsentience, which are determined by whether what you're sensing is animate or inanimate. The first aspect, clairempathy, is the ability to feel the emotions and energy of people and living things (animate). The other, clairtangency or psychometry, is the ability to feel the energy and emotions of objects and places (inanimate).

In the context of mediumship, clairsentience can be used to provide evidential information about the person in Spirit, by feeling that information in your own body. For example, you can feel their size or height, how they carried themselves (slouchy or book-on-the-head posture), what they did for a living (feeling the energy in your head or in your hands), their overall personality and emotions and even how they died. All this information is conveyed through your body and emotions.

Some people report feeling clairsentience in their solar plexus as a sense of knowing on an emotional level (rather than on a mental level as a flash of clarity or knowing, which is claircognizance). Or you might feel it around your heart center. This is because the chakras associated with clairsentience are your heart, solar plexus and sacral chakras.

Clairsentience developing exercises

You may feel physical sensations in your body that relate to the person in Spirit you are connecting with.

You might experience clairsentience as a nudging, tapping or pulling (like a magnetic pull), as if to get your attention about a physical object or person.

You may feel clairsentience as a push/pull, or restriction/flow of energy. There are many times when I find myself playing what I call 20 Questions with Spirit and feeling for the answer. Is it this? Yes/no. Is it that? Yes/no. This happens very quickly and behind the scenes, as I pose these questions and intuitively receive the answers along with other associated impressions.

Clairsentience is often combined with other intuitive senses, such as clairvoyance, clairaudience, clairgustance or clairalience to give clearer information and understanding of what's coming through. Clairsentience is also closely tied to empathy, and people who are empaths often have a strong connection to their clairsentience.

The following exercises will help you tune into how you feel clairsentience in your body.

Send and receive emotions

Emotions are energetically sensed and felt through clairsentience and can give a lot of useful information about the people in Spirit you connect with.

This exercise helps you practice sensing the projected emotions of others.

How to do the exercise

There are two ways to do this exercise: in pairs or in a circle format. Either way, the basic premise is the same. When it's each person's turn to go, they choose an emotion to focus on and send to the receiver(s).

The receiver(s) open themselves to receiving the emotional information and make note of whatever it is they get.

It's helpful to use a pre-selected range of emotions or feelings, rather than to have each sender choose the emotion they send. This randomizes the selection and makes it more specific and concrete.

One way to do this is to use a card deck, such as James Van Praagh's *The Power of Love Activation Cards*. Not all of the words on the cards will be applicable or able to be easily sent, so go through the deck and create a stack of cards with emotions and remove cards that don't apply. One of the benefits of using a card deck is that there are usually explanatory words that go along with the feeling or emotional state on the card which people often tend to pick up on as well.

You can also create your own version on slips of paper.

Clairsentience exercises – Send and receive emotions

Some suggestions for emotions or feeling states are:

- Integrity
- Ownership
- Willingness
- Virtue
- Loyalty
- Tolerance
- Transformation
- Satisfaction
- Relief
- Purpose
- Kindness
- Distrust
- Commitment
- Joy
- Unity
- Self-love
- Grateful
- Harmony
- Humility
- Individuality
- Cooperation
- Freedom

- Compassion
- Hurt
- Trusting
- Fearful
- Patience
- Friendly
- Forgiveness
- Acceptance
- Empathy
- Peacefulness
- Creative
- Detached
- Visionary
- Respect
- Responsible
- Movement
- Grounded
- Positive
- Negative
- Despair
- Depression
- Healing

Clairsentience exercises – Send and receive emotions

- Strong
- Weak
- Focused
- Energetic
- Tired
- Protective
- Calm
- Busy
- Frustrated
- Angry
- Proud
- Ashamed
- Balanced
- Off-kilter
- Abundant
- Lonely
- Loving

In pairs

- Break into pairs, with each partner sitting across from each other.
- Decide who'll be the sender and who'll be the receiver.
- The sender chooses an emotion or feeling to focus on.
- Both people close their eyes and take a few cleansing breaths.
- The sender projects the emotion or feeling directly to the receiver. Don't try too hard or make great effort. Embody the emotion within yourself.
- The receiver notices the impressions they receive and writes them down (or remembers them).
- After about a minute or two, at the most, the receiver shares what they got with the sender and the sender shares what the emotion was.

Clairsentience exercises – Send and receive emotions

- Both partners take several deep, cleansing breaths to release the emotion.
- The partners switch roles.
- Once each partner has had a turn, switch partners or choose a new card with your current partner and go again.

In a circle

- The circle members take turns going around the circle, with one person sending an emotion and the rest of the circle receiving and writing down, or remembering, their impressions.
- After a minute or two at the most, circle members share what they got.
- When all members have shared their impressions, the receiver shares the emotion they were sending.
- Everyone in the circle takes three deep, cleansing breaths (in through the nose, out through the mouth) to release the emotion.
- The next person in the circle becomes the sender and this continues until each person in the circle has had a turn being the sender.

Online

In order to be able to do this online, each circle member needs to have a set of cards or words to choose from. Once you've accomplished that, you can practice this exercise in the same way as you would in-person, either as a circle on in pairs in breakout rooms.

The sender chooses one of their cards to focus on while the rest of the circle members or the partner receive the information for a minute or two, then share what they got.

The takeaway

This exercise teaches you several things, one of the most important being trust in yourself and your connection with Spirit. It can feel hard to share what you receive and you might feel like you're going to make a fool of yourself. It's OK. Your development circle is a safe place where you can be vulnerable and open. You don't need to be right. There's no scorecard here.

It also teaches you how you feel these different emotions in your body and through your intuitive senses. What did the emotions that you received, and the emotion that you sent, feel like? How did they come through? Notice that and take note of it in a journal or symbol workbook. The ways you received information may be the way these emotions come through for your symbolically.

Finally, this exercise helps you develop your clairsentience abilities, simply by using them. Your intuitive senses are like muscles that need exercise in order to gain strength, clarity and stamina.

Sense the presence of others

When you connect to people in Spirit, one of your goals is to determine who it is that you're communicating with. Are they male, female or neither? Are they old or young, tall or short, heavyset or slender?

While this sensation is most often experienced in your body, it's hard to explain what it feels like. The best way to learn the physical characteristics of your Spirit communicator—such as the gender, age, height, body type and weight, clothing, and skin, hair and eye color—is to experience it yourself.

All of the characteristics a person has are part of what forms their energy signature. Every person has a unique energy signature. This exercise helps you feel and tune into the energy signature of the people in your development circle.

When you do the exercise, you can first start by asking if they are male, female, non-binary or agender, then move on to other things about them in order to determine who they are. This helps you learn what those different characteristics feel like on an intuitive or psychic level. You'll then be better able to differentiate the characteristics of your Spirit communicators.

How to do the exercise

You'll need a room large enough that one of your circle members can sit several feet away from the other circle members.

The person actively doing the sensing and tuning in sits in a chair at one end of the room. You can blindfold them, or not, depending on your preference. If they don't wear a blindfold, they should close their eyes.

Clairsentience exercises – Sense the presence of others

The other circle members cluster together on the other side of the room.

- One at a time, each person quietly steps forward, in random order, into the energy field of the person in the chair.

- The circle leader announces: "The first person has stepped forward," to ensure that the person in the chair knows there's a presence behind them to sense.

- Allow the person in the chair time to sense information about the person standing behind them—up to two or three minutes maximum, as first impressions are often the most accurate. They can sense for one or two of the physical characteristics or for the person as a whole.

- When the person in the chair is ready for the person standing behind them to step back, they can signal in some way, perhaps by saying, "OK," or raising a hand. At this point, they can either give whatever information they received, or they can make a note of it on a pad on their lap. (It would help to not be blindfolded if they are going to write.)

- The person standing behind them steps back into the group as the group's spokesperson says, "The first person is stepping back."

- The next person steps forward as the circle leader says, "The second person is stepping forward."

- Repeat the process through all the circle members.

- During this, the circle leader should make a note of the order of who stepped forward when, to keep track. If the person in the chair is sharing the information they

Clairsentience exercises – Sense the presence of others

received as each person steps forward, also make a note of what they say.

- When you've gone through the whole circle stepping forward and back, share the results with the person in the chair as far as their accuracy and impressions.

- Switch who sits in the chair and repeat again, until each member of the circle has had a chance to sit in the chair.

Online

There isn't really a great way to do this exercise in an online format, but if you think of one, let me know!

The Takeaway

It really doesn't matter what you get. You don't have to be accurate. You may be, and some people will likely be more accurate than others. But it really doesn't matter.

The whole idea is for you to begin sensing and understanding how to connect with an energy signature and how different characteristics feel in your body when you do. This will help you identify Spirit communicators when you do readings.

If you were able to correctly get information about or tell the identity of the people who stood behind you, that's wonderful. Now you know how those characteristics feel or show up for you.

If you didn't correctly identify people, that's great, too. Because now you have feedback about the information you sensed and received and can use that feedback the next time you connect. When that's been the case for my students, they usually got a sense that they weren't truly listening to their intuition and second-guessed themselves or were overthinking their impressions. This is an important signal to learn, so you can begin to trust what you get.

Go inward into your body

Your body is a useful and accurate tool to provide you intuitive clairsentient information. Its information usually comes in a binary language—a flow or resistance of energy—and is most often felt in the solar plexus and sacral chakras, but can also be felt in your heart center, your root, and even your feet.

To access this information easily, you need to allow your sense of yourself to really live in your body. A lot of times with mediumship, especially when you're connecting with information that you believe is outside yourself, you project your consciousness outside of your physical body. There's a huge tendency to want to play in Spirit, to raise your vibration up to the level of Spirit, to talk to your guides as if they were "up there" somewhere, or to experience astral travel and out of body experiences. There's not necessarily anything wrong with this, but it can disconnect you from your physical self, which can be detrimental to your health.

In order to experience this lifetime, you need a physical body, so you can have a physical experience as well as a spiritual one. Maintaining your connection to your physical body is important. Rather than reaching outside yourself to connect with information from Spirit, allow that information to come to you and through you. This helps you stay grounded and more easily get rid of excess energy. Plus, it helps you better discern the difference between information that's coming from you and what's coming from Spirit.

Clairsentience exercises – Go inward into your body

How to do the exercise

This exercise is done in a circle, as a guided meditation, with one member of the circle leading the others in the meditation.

- Guide the circle into a meditative state, then use the following script.
- Bring your awareness into your physical body. Notice where your awareness first rests—your heart, your gut, your head, your pelvis?
- Take several breaths to scan your body from head to toe. Notice what it feels like in the different areas of your body.
- Are there areas of restriction or discomfort? Are there areas that feel free, clear and contented? Just notice.
- You don't need to make any judgments or ask any questions. As thoughts about what you're experiencing come up, notice them and let them go.
- Now take a step inward into your physical self.
- Imagine your body as if it is a fractal—no matter how deep you go, there is more there, working and humming away in harmony. Your body knows what it needs to do to keep itself running.
- Feel your heart beating without any effort or consciousness on your part.
- Allow your lungs to take in and release air easily and naturally.
- Sense the nerves running throughout your body sending signals, allowing you to feel the chair you're sitting on.

- Notice the sensation of your breath moving in and out of your nose and lungs.
- Sense the blood vessels and veins taking oxygen from the air, through your lungs, into every cell of your body.
- Within your organs there are cells. Within the cells there are atoms. Within each of the millions of atoms there is vast space. All of that is Spirit. All of it is Infinite Intelligence.
- See how deep you can go into the experience of your physical self.
- Ask your body: Is there anything I need to know right now? Trust what you get.
- When you're ready, bring your awareness back up to the surface level of being in your body.
- Do another body scan. Does anything feel different?
- Where does your sense of your awareness rest now?
- Take one or two more deep breaths, wiggle your fingers and toes, and open your eyes.
- After the meditation, share your experiences and any messages you received from the infinite spaces of your inner body.

Online

You follow the same format, whether you're meeting in person or online.

The takeaway

The more you're able to tune into your body and feel its normal resting state, the easier it is for you to know when

Clairsentience exercises – Go inward into your body

something is out of balance, or when your body is communicating intuitively with you.

A good connection with your physical body helps you stay healthy, in terms of understanding what your body needs (or doesn't need). It also protects you from unwanted energy from others, especially energy and emotions that don't feel good. Many clairsentient people are empaths and tend to pick up the energy and emotions of the people and places around them.

Being grounded and connected to your body protects you from that, by giving you a stronger sense of what energy is yours and what's not yours and making it easier to shed what's not yours, like water off a duck's back, as the saying goes. This is vitally important in being healthy, physically and emotionally.

Extend your awareness

This exercise is similar to tuning into your body, but extends your awareness outside of your body into the world around you, while you remain grounded and centered.

Some people would describe this as extending your aura or auric field.

It's likely you extend your intuitive senses or aura outside yourself already, so it's good to learn to discern when you're doing this, so you can be in control of it. This helps you develop control over your clairsentience.

As you learn to determine what energy is yours and what's not yours, you become more protected from unwanted energy from other people.

How to do the exercise

This is a guided meditation that one person in the group should lead the others in.

- Guide the circle into a quiet meditative state, then follow the script below.
- Allow your awareness to rest within your physical body, perhaps in your heart center or solar plexus.
- Do a scan of your body, just noticing how your body is feeling. You don't need to solve or fix anything at all. Just notice it and let it be.
- Imagine your sense of self, your awareness, as if it is a sphere of light in your heart or solar plexus. It can be any

Clairsentience exercises – Extend your awareness

color you like, whatever first comes up. Don't over think it.

- Get a sense of how your own energy feels. How would you identify your own energy signature? What does your sense of your physical self feel like?
- Now allow your intuitive sense of self to expand.
- Imagine the sphere of light that is your awareness getting bigger and bigger, encompassing more of the room around you.
- What do you feel? Can you sense the energy of the objects or people around you?
- Be gentle. Don't push too far or too fast. If it feels uncomfortable, stop a moment and breathe, just like you would if you were stretching a tight muscle. Relax into it through your breath.
- If you get physical sensations that you find unpleasant, make sure your feet are grounded into the Earth and back off a little. When you feel centered and clear, extend your awareness a little more.
- Continue to make the sphere of your awareness as big as you'd like—whether that's four feet away from you or encompassing the building you're in and half the block, or even further.
- As you extend your awareness further outward from yourself, notice how the information changes. Does it stay the same strength or does it seem diluted?
- After a few minutes, begin to contract your awareness back into your own physical self.

Clairsentience exercises – Extend your awareness

- Do this with your breath. As you exhale, feel your physical body contract as your lungs empty, and bring your clairsentient sense back in with your breath.
- As you inhale, ground yourself.
- Take as many breaths as you need until you feel your energy within your own body.
- Once your sense of self is back in your physical center, take a few breaths here to settle and center yourself again.
- Notice once more the difference in your own energy compared to the energy around you.
- Sit with your own energy for a few more breaths.
- Begin to become aware of the sounds in the room around you, the sensation of air on your skin, the weight of your body in the seat, your feet on the floor and your hands in your lap.
- Wiggle your fingers and toes and gently open your eyes.

After the exercise, share what the experience was like for each member of the circle.

Consider these questions:

- What did your own energy feel like?
- What was it like when you extended your energy outside of yourself?
- How did the quality of the energetic information change as your awareness extended further and further from yourself?

Clairsentience exercises – Extend your awareness

Online

The format is the same whether you do this online or in-person.

The takeaway

Learning to know where your awareness is and where the energy you're picking up is coming from is extremely important in being able to know what's yours and what's not yours. This helps you with clarity and accuracy in your message work.

It also helps you to not get overwhelmed by the clairsentient information you connect with. Clairsentience is a wonderful ability, but it can sometimes feel like a curse. Picking up other people's energy, when you don't mean to, is easily overwhelming and often unpleasant. Knowing what your own energy feels like helps you know when you're getting something different. Also, being aware of how far you're extending your own aura helps you better stay grounded and keep your own energy within yourself.

The next time you're out and about and you find yourself picking up other people's energy or thoughts, check your auric field. Where is your awareness?

Get information through your energy centers

Another way you can use clairsentience is to allow the information to come to you and flow through your energy centers, rather than extend your awareness outside of yourself. This may be a preferable way of accessing this ability if you tend to get overwhelmed with the cares and worries of the world and other people's energy.

Allowing the information to come to you in this way allows you to be more grounded and come from a place of strength, plus it actually helps you to stay more balanced and centered.

When you use your physical senses, you don't extend your eyeballs or ears out to the thing you're seeing or hearing. You let the information (through the form of light waves or sound waves) come to you, where you take it into your body and process it into information you can understand and use. Getting clairsentient information can be done in the same way.

Imagine your heart, solar plexus and sacral chakras as the receptors of this energetic information and let them take it in, filter it and turn it into useful information for you.

How to do the exercise

It may be helpful to have some music playing as you do this exercise, although it can also be done in silence.

It can either be led as a guided exercise, or the circle leader can explain it to the members at the beginning of the exercise and everyone can go at their own pace, with the circle leader only guiding everyone else in and out of the exercise.

Clairsentience exercises – Use your energy centers

- Sit quietly and allow yourself to get into a meditative state.
- Begin to breathe the energy of the room around you.
- Imagine it filtering in through your sacral, solar plexus and heart chakras.
- Notice how the information comes through—perhaps as pulses, colors or smells. Or an internal sense of rightness or wrongness.
- Just notice it and be with whatever comes up.
- While keeping your awareness in your body, focus it on another person in your circle. Think of it like looking at the person—your eyes don't leave your body, they just focus on the person while staying in your head. Use your chakras to focus on the person, without extending your awareness or aura out to them.
- Allow their energy to come in through your energy centers.
- Notice how the information comes through and what it feels like to you.
- Either make a mental or written note of the information you receive—any impressions, feelings or messages.
- Turn your focus back to yourself and imagine your sacral, solar plexus and heart chakras as spinning wheels, clear and bright, releasing any energy you picked up.
- Now focus on another person in the circle, again keeping your awareness inside your body and allowing their energy to come in through your chakras.

- Continue this process around the circle until you've focused on each person, bringing your focus back to yourself and clearing out or releasing the energy from your chakras each time.
- After this exercise, each person shares the information and impressions they received.

A variation

An alternate option is to focus on loved ones in Spirit, either your own loved ones or other circle members, and focus on them through these chakras.

Online

This exercise is done the same whether you're meeting in person or online.

The takeaway

If you're used to extending out from yourself to get information, this way of getting information may take some getting used to. However, it's an extremely worthwhile method. This exercise teaches you to sit in your own power, allowing information to come to you, rather than going out to get it.

If you had a difficult childhood and learned to protect yourself by assessing the emotions and probable reactions of the people around you, you may have learned to use your clairsentient abilities by extending your awareness. It's sort of like feeling out the emotional temperature of a room before stepping into it. That was a wonderful survival mechanism, but it's not a healthy way to be in the world all the time.

Extending your awareness outward from yourself tends to leave you exhausted and overwhelmed. By allowing energetic information to come to you, and keeping your own chakras clear, you're protected and grounded.

Psychometry: sense the energy of objects

Psychometry is the ability to sense the energy of an object or place. It's the clairtangency (clear touch) aspect of clairsentience.

Everything in the universe vibrates at its own particular frequency, including you. When you're in close contact with objects and places, you tend to leave some of your energy signature behind as impressions.

This is especially true for the things that have emotional meaning to you and that you come into close contact with over time, such as jewelry.

This imprinting of energy onto objects allows you to tune into the object owner's frequency and learn about them, as well as the history of the object. You use the object both as a way to connect with the energy of the owner and to access the energetic information stored in the object itself.

How to do the exercise

To do this exercise, you'll need objects that are meaningful to you or to a friend or loved one.

- Each circle member brings an object of meaning to them to the circle. It should be small enough to fit into a bowl or basket and be something they know the history of or keep close to them. Examples of objects that tend to work well include jewelry, mementoes, a small gift given by a loved one who's now in Spirit, a stone or crystal you keep in your pocket, etc.
- Don't show this object to the other circle members.

Clairsentience exercises – Psychometry

- At the beginning of the circle, each person places their object in a bowl under a covered cloth.

- When you're ready to begin the exercise, pass the bowl around and have each person take someone else's object. If they get their own object, they put it back and pick another one.

- You can choose to look at or not look at the object you pick. If you're feeling courageous enough, try the exercise without looking at the object, as it removes one level of assumption your rational mind will make about the object, who owns it and what it means.

- Go into a meditative state as a circle.

- Hold the object in your hand and extend your awareness into it and allow its energy to flow into you.

- Allow impressions to come to you. Don't discard any of them, no matter how odd or silly they may seem. Just take note of them. Information may come through any of your intuitive senses—you may feel emotions, see images, hear sounds, smell something or even get a taste of food or another substance.

- Either while you're still sensing the object or right afterwards, write down what you experienced if you find that helpful.

- After the meditation, go around the circle and take turns sharing what you got. See if you can tell who the object belongs to.

- At the end of your sharing, the object's owner speaks up to claim it and offer confirmation about the information and message you gave.

Online

- Each circle member asks a friend or loved one for an object that is meaningful to its owner. If you don't want to look at the object, put it in an envelope until it's time for your circle to meet.

- During the circle, each person takes out the object they've procured and tunes into it during the meditation, just like you would in an in-person circle.

- Since the object's owner isn't around, it's a good idea to take a few minutes to write down your impressions afterward.

- Then take turns sharing what you got with the rest of the circle. As none of the objects will belong to any other circle member, they can't confirm the information you share, but that's OK. You can later share your impressions with the object's owner. For now, just share with your circle members, as the act of speaking the information you received helps to make the connection and your confidence stronger.

The takeaway

It really doesn't matter how accurate you are with this exercise, especially to begin with.

If the impressions you get don't connect with what the object owner knows about the object, keep these things in mind:

- Symbols, especially ones received visually, are sometimes literal and sometimes metaphorical.

- If the symbols are metaphorical, what they mean may not be what you initially think they do. Dig deeper into the

Clairsentience exercises – Psychometry

symbol and see if you can get to the hidden layers of information about it.

- Sometimes, your own experiences (especially difficult ones) that are somehow associated with the object or triggered by the object can color your impressions and reading of its energy. This can be more prevalent when you first start practicing mediumship, as you haven't yet learned to take an emotional step back from the energy you're sensing.

The act of trust, opening up and relaying the information that comes through is the essential part of this exercise. The owner of the object may not know everything about it, or something may be getting lost in translation as you give them the information. There are lots of potential variables at play. Just trust what comes up and give it as clearly as you get it, then let it go. It's all about the practice.

Medical intuition

The idea of this exercise is to practice sensing what's going on in another person's body on several different levels: physical, emotional and spiritual.

We store a lot of information from the past in our body and this can affect our present health. Past physical injuries and surgeries leave scars. Painful emotional experiences are also stored in our body and can use pain as a way of getting our attention. And sometimes we carry information from other lifetimes, so that it can come up to be resolved now.

How to do the exercise

This exercise is most easily done in an in-person circle, especially if you have a massage table so you can take turns lying down on it, allowing the rest of the circle to use their hands to sense energy.

But it can also be done in a seated circle and online.

With a massage table

- If you have a massage table, have the first participant lie down on it. You can also potentially use the floor, a table or couch, they'll just be a bit less comfortable and it will be more awkward for the other circle members.

- The other circle members should scan the participant lying down. You can all do this at the same time, or take turns.

- You can use your hands, hovering them a few inches above their body, without touching them, as an additional way of picking up energy.

Clairsentience exercises – Medical intuition

- What do you sense? Do you get areas of heat or cold? Are there areas of the body your hands or eyes are drawn to? Do you get information within your own body?
- After a few minutes, share your impressions, then switch to another circle member lying down on the massage table.

Without a massage table and/or online

If you're not using a massage table, the directions are the same whether you are meeting in person or online.

- Choose one participant to go first. Have them sit quietly, with their arms and legs uncrossed.
- (If you're online, have that person's web cam feed be the dominant one on the screen.)
- The other circle members focus on the volunteer sitter's body, scanning it to see what areas catch their attention.
- Because I also do energy healing work, I find it helpful to close my eyes and visualize moving my hands over their body (as if I was doing energy healing) in my mind's eye. This allows me to pick up energetic information in my hands.
- You may also feel the information within your own body as areas of warmth or cold, restriction or tenseness.
- After a few minutes, the circle members sending information share what they got with the sitter.
- Then switch to another person in the circle as the sitter until you go through each of the people in your circle.

The takeaway

This exercise is useful for people wishing to develop their medical intuition skills.

The body holds a lot of information. The impressions you get with this exercise are often in the form of feeling what's right or wrong with the body, its organs and systems. For instance, you might feel pressure, weight, restriction or heat in the abdomen around the area of the liver, perhaps. Your intuition may then show you images or feelings around what that might mean.

Be careful not to diagnose or prescribe when doing this exercise. You don't want to cause someone to believe they have cancer, for instance. But you could share that you feel an area of heat in the breast, perhaps.

Remember that many physical illnesses and issues have emotional causes. The same is true for the energetic information you might get. So the kidney may signify worries about money, the liver a feeling of being stuck or in a toxic situation, the chest emotional burdens or worries, rather than being physical issues in these organs or areas.

Use your best judgement in how you share the information you get with this exercise.

Play intuitive Q&A

This exercise teaches you how to use your body to get answers to someone's questions. You'll learn how to sense the yes/no/maybe feeling within your physical self, what that energy is like, and how it's different from the information your brain gives you.

It also gives you some experience in doing an intuitive reading for a client and being able to answer their questions about their path forward. (While this book is about mediumship development, if you go on to practice professionally, many clients will ask you for psychic or intuitive information about their lives as well as a connection to their loved ones via mediumship.)

How to do the exercise

This exercise is done in pairs.

- Sit across from your partner, arms and legs uncrossed.
- Choose which partner is going to ask questions first and who'll give intuitively-guided answers.
- Take a few deep breaths to relax and open your energy and bring you into the present moment.
- The sitter begins by asking a question related to them. Questions can be about any aspect of your life: health, career, romance, finances, moving/housing, etc. Whatever you're curious about or are currently working through.

Clairsentience exercises – Play intuitive Q&A

- Begin with small specific questions that have a yes/no answer. E.g. *Are strawberries good for me? Should I start practicing yoga?*
- The other person sits quietly and feels what comes up for them in their body. Is there a feeling of expansion or contraction? A spark of energy or a sinking feeling? A flow or a stop?
- They can describe what they're getting for each question, how the sensations feel. Or they can interpret them as a yes, no, or maybe response. It depends on whether they are able to make a strong connection to the sensation or not.
- The sitter continues asking questions for several minutes.
- Then partners switch roles.

Online

Pairing up online is a little tricky, but can be done using breakout rooms. Once you've paired up, follow the instructions above.

The takeaway

This exercise helps you learn how information can come through your body in a binary yes/no way.

It also gives you the opportunity to notice how your brain reacts differently from your body. For instance, if the sitter asks, "Are strawberries good for me?" your brain may immediately think, "Yes, of course they are. Strawberries are a healthy fruit!" But your body may give you different information. Or perhaps you have an aversion to strawberries and so you begin to think,

Clairsentience exercises – Play intuitive Q&A

"Yuck! Strawberries. Ugh." But your body gives you a spark or flow or energy.

Similarly, the sitter might ask, "Should I move to Arizona?" and you get a tug of sadness in your heart as you think of your circle member leaving. However, the intuitive information you receive through your body feels different.

In mediumship work, it's important to learn not only to take ourselves out of the equation, but to notice when we're accidentally responding from our own biases. We all have biases, there's no way around them, other than to become aware of them and what it feels like when they get activated.

This is especially important with clairsentience, as you're essentially using your physical body as an instrument. Getting the calibration right, and adjusting for interference (from your mind or emotions) is important.

Physical mediumship

Physical mediumship is not something to be entered into lightly. A circle that sits for physical mediumship might sit and work for weeks or months before they experience any physical phenomena.

It's best that you have a medium leading your circle who has experienced physical mediumship before to lead you in developing it for your circle.

That said, physical mediumship can be a lot of fun, so I'm including a few exercises that you can try and will be most likely to have success with, given the patience and willingness to keep trying.

In my own attempts at physical mediumship, I've found that keeping your spirits up and the energy high helps a lot. Be willing to be amazed. Have a beginner's mind and be open to wonder.

The following explanation and the exercises on spoon bending, table tipping and pendulum dowsing are excerpts from my book on physical mediumship: *Spirit Energy: Table tipping, trumpet voices, trance channeling and other phenomena of physical mediumship*. Because of this, their explanations and format vary from the previous exercises.

How physical mediumship works

Physical mediumship is different from mental mediumship in that mental mediumship comes primarily through your mind and physical mediumship goes through your body.

While some aspects of mental mediumship, such as clairsentience, can feel quite physical and use your intuitive body and its energy centers to receive and information, it's the connection with your brain that interprets the information and makes sense of it. Your ears may be a physical feature that hear soundwaves, but your brain interprets them into meaning, whether that's the sound of a word, a baby's cry or a bird call. Even clairsentience and the push and pull of energy or the seeming physical sensations of how someone died aren't truly physical.

In physical mediumship, the manifestations themselves are usually of a physical nature, which can be independently and objectively observed—such as a table tipping, direct voice and materialization—or they come through the physical body without using the medium's mental faculties to make them occur—such as automatic writing and trance channeling.

To produce physical mediumship, the medium's physical body needs to be a good conduit for these physical manifestations.

What makes a good physical conduit? According to Clifford Bias in his booklet *Physical Mediumship*, there needs to be "a plentiful source of etheric energy," which is furnished by the sitters and the medium that the medium is then able to make available for the Spirit entities to use to produce physical phenomena.

Bias suggests that a medium can test whether or not they might have a plentiful supply of etheric energy by doing some light exercises, raising up and down on their toes several times, then bending backward and forward with their hands on their hips until they experience a "glow" or feeling of exhilaration. At that point, while standing in front of a mirror in a dimly lit room, they can rub their hands together, press their fingertips together and then draw them apart, watching their reflection in the mirror.

"A 'stream' of etheric substance can be seen (if you have a superabundance of it) connecting the fingers," Bias writes. It will be barely visible and faint electric blue or peach in color. (*Physical Mediumship*, p. 11)

Ectoplasm

If you've studied physical mediumship at all, you've probably heard of ectoplasm—the mysterious substance that makes it possible.

The reason that having lots of etheric energy is important in physical mediumship is because it's used to produce ectoplasm.

Bias describes ectoplasm as "a semi-physical, semi-etheric substance" that is actually "'physicalized' etheric matter." (*Physical Mediumship*, p. 14)

In *Mediumship and Its Phases*, Margaret L. King describes ectoplasm as "matter invisible and intangible in its primary state but assuming vaporous, liquid or solid condition in its various stages of condensation." (p. 31)

Bias agrees that ectoplasm can vary in appearance and density—it can be invisible, a misty gas, a "viscous gelatin like fluid," a soft lacy material or a hard solid. (*Physical Mediumship*,

p. 14) I've also heard it described as "Spirit snot," as it's often mucousy.

In color, Bias says it's usually pale—white, grey or pastel—although sometimes black, but rarely a bright color.

The word ectoplasm was coined by Charles Richet, a French physiologist, in 1894.

Physical mediums exude etheric energy and ectoplasm from their solar plexus and orifices (yes, all of them) which is then used by Spirit to form the supports that move tables around, levitate people, create voice boxes for trumpet mediumship, and materialize as the face of a loved one in Spirit.

When practicing physical mediumship, ectoplasm and etheric energy comes not only from the medium, but from everyone present. Some people say that the medium's doctor or chemist Spirit guide uses the etheric energy to alter the chemistry of the medium's body to produce ectoplasm. However, if your belief is (like mine) that your Spirit guides are really aspects of your own higher self, rather than separate entities, then it's your own inner wisdom making any such changes to produce ectoplasm, rather than an external force.

Generally, the dominant physical medium in the group not only produces etheric energy, but draws energy from the other sitters, centers it within themselves and turns it into ectoplasm for Spirit to then produce physical phenomena with. The precise method of how this happens seems unknown.

A Spirit control

The other aspect of physical mediumship is working with an entity in Spirit, who understands how to manipulate the ectoplasm produced by the medium and sitters, and how to turn it into physical manifestations of whatever sort.

What kind of Spirit control are you likely to get as you develop physical mediumship? Well, just as with mental mediumship, the laws of vibration and attraction come into play. This means you're going to attract someone in Spirit who is harmonious with you and has an affinity for your energy.

Table tipping

Table tipping used to be a popular way to manifest physical Spiritualist phenomena. I consider it to be a fun way to connect with Spirit and expand your mind and acceptance of what may be possible.

There are several theories about how table tipping actually works.

Rods made of ectoplasm is a common theory. King writes in *Mediumship and Its Phases* that "ectoplasm rods are formed in sufficient strength for spirit forces to bring about the rapping or table tipping." (p. 31) Bias considers the movement to be caused by the etheric energy of those present.

Skeptics say that it's really the unconscious minds of the sitters at work, causing small movements in the muscles of their hands and arms that make the table move. This is caused by the ideomotor response, which I'll cover more in the chapter on dowsing and pendulums.

Bias agrees that this can be case, as "the dominant or most active mind in the room, either incarnate or discarnate, can direct the motions of the table." (*Physical Mediumship*, p. 14) This most active mind can be that of someone in Spirit. But, if you don't know how to connect with Spirit, then it could possibly be "the conscious or unconscious desire of one or more of those present." That's why you should develop mental mediumship abilities first, so you can connect with Spirit.

In my own experience, I've seen the table move more than seems reasonable if it were just the sitters at work, consciously or not. I've even taken video of it and asked the sitters to move their hands so that you can clearly see that no one is actually moving the table.

There have also been reports of tables being tilted on two or one legs and even climbing the walls and levitating, which seems more of a stretch to believe that it's caused by our own unconscious desires than it is to believe it's Spirit at work.

How to practice table tipping

While some mediums can produce table tipping phenomena alone, it's best to have the combined energy of several people. If your circle decides to practice this, be prepared to work at it for several weeks before anything exciting happens.

The table

First, you need a table. Many sources suggest a small, round, three-legged wooden table. In my experience, it doesn't have to be any of those things, except wooden. Smaller is better to start with than huge and heavy, as it will take less etheric energy or ectoplasm to move it and producing ectoplasm is a bit like getting any muscle in shape. You want to start small and light-weight.

The number of legs doesn't matter, either. I've done table tipping with a four-legged table with no issues. And a square or a rectangular table works just as well as a round one.

You either want the table to be large enough or the number of people to be few enough that you all fit around the table without being squished while leaving the table room to move.

Some people recommend cleansing the table to release residual energy attached to it, which you can do by spraying it with salt water and wiping it off or by smudging it with sage smoke. You may also want to say a brief prayer, dedicating the table to Spirit's use. I've also used tables that I used for other things in my home, but it's nice if you can have a dedicated table for table tipping, especially to start.

The room

The room can be lit however you want. Some mediums like it to be completely dark, others do table tipping demonstrations in well-lit auditoriums. I suggest making it dim to start. If it's daytime, draw the shades. If it's night time, have a low lamp on so everyone can see, but without it being too bright. You can have a lit candle nearby and many Spiritualists suggest having a glass or bowl of water in the room to help facilitate communication with Spirit.

Hand placement

Instructions for the placement of your hands varies. Some, such as Bias, advocate for placing the hands palm down, flat on the table, with each person's thumbs touching and their little fingers touching that of the person next to them. In theory, this creates a ring or circuit through which energy can pass from one person to the next. In practice, I find it uncomfortable and prefer a little space between each person's hands.

I've also done table tipping—and have been instructed by Spirit during a table tipping session—to have our fingertips underneath the table. Listen to your guides and inner knowing.

However you place your hands, keep the pressure as light as you can. You want to make a connection with the table, but not press on it at all.

How to start

When you're ready to start a session, have everyone sit around the table and open with a prayer.

After you've opened with a prayer and asked your guides to step in to help you have a successful and wonderful experience, raise the vibration by singing. Pick songs everyone knows—old standards such as "Row, Row, Row the Boat" are fine, even if you feel silly. Well-known hymns work as well. Sing a few songs, and then sit in meditation and open yourself to the experience.

What to expect

What can you expect to happen? Possibly a number of things.

In *The Art of Mediumship: Psychic Investigation, Clairvoyance and Channeling*, Elaine Kuzmeskus, writes, "With regular practice, your fingers will begin to feel sticky as if they are melding into the table. This is a sure sign that you are making progress. Soon the table should vibrate a bit...With practice, it will move back and forth." (p. 126)

As Bias writes, "In a few moments, the table seems to become 'alive'; those whose hands are on the table can feel an undulation, a sort of pulsation or internal movement in it. Then it moves—it tilts on two or even one leg. It rocks back and forth, it turns in a circle, it slides along the floor." (*Physical Mediumship*, p. 12)

Before the table moves, you should feel a build-up or movement or energy within your solar plexus. If you're the most experienced medium, you may feel a drawing sensation both from and into your solar plexus, as if you are drawing in the etheric energy of the other sitters and using it to create ectoplasm. You may feel a shuddering or vibration in your arms or hands, as if energy is moving through you into the table.

In one experience I had, one of my hands started vibrating and moving, as if it wanted to move the table. In this instance, I consciously relaxed my physical body to let the energy flow through me.

If you're not the most experienced medium in the circle, you may feel a drawing of energy from your solar plexus, either into the table itself or the head medium.

You may also hear raps or creaks coming from the table before it physically moves, tilts or turns. Or you may get the sense of it vibrating.

What to do if nothing happens

If you've said your opening prayer and sung a few songs and nothing seems to be happening here are some things you can try:

- Practice sending energy to the person across the table from you.
- Give the table a physical jiggle or shake—it can be helpful psychologically to know the table can actually move and has not, somehow, become glued to the floor.
- Change your hand placement if that feels right—if your hands were under the table, try putting them on top of the table.
- Relax—notice the tension you're holding in your hands and arms, take a good, deep breath and relax.
- Ask or tell the table to start moving.

- Ask Spirit for instruction—ask your guides or any friendly entities in Spirit for instruction on how to move forward successfully.

What to do when things start happening

When the table starts moving, it's awesome. You'll gasp and laugh. The energy is uplifting and exhilarating. It feels really good. Smile and feel glad within your heart.

Next, it's time to establish a baseline for communication. You can do this in several ways, so choose what feels right for you.

The way I've typically done it is to establish what means *yes* and what means *no*. For instance, clockwise movement means *yes* and counterclockwise rotation means *no*. Or moving to the left and right means one thing and moving up and down—in relation to one of the sitters—means the other. If the table is tilting on two legs, perhaps that can mean *yes*, and if it tilts on the opposite two legs, that can mean *no*. You get the idea.

Some mediums prefer to use the letters of the alphabet to spell out messages, but I think that takes too long and prefer to rely on my mental mediumship to get more detailed or nuanced answers as needed.

Once you've established how you're communicating, you can ask questions—about pretty much anything, always understanding you'll receive only your highest good. You can ask who the Spirit entity is: their name, dates of birth and death, if they were male or female, etc. With yes/no questions, this can require a lot of questions and answers to pin some things down, so decide for yourself what you want to know.

You can also ask questions about your life and your future path. At one table tipping session, I was told I was going to have two more children who'd be twins (I was pregnant with my second child at the time, so I was aghast at this news), but I'd have enough help to cope with it all and my husband would have a good job so we could afford it. I was also told I'd move to the West Coast around the time my oldest was going to Kindergarten. I still have my notes from the session somewhere in one of my many journals where I tucked it afterward.

It turns out I did move to the West Coast when my oldest was four and going into pre-K and I did end up with two more children at the same time—my step-children, who have biological parents of their own to help take care of them, one of whom is their dad who has a good job.

You never know how things are going to turn out, so ask for your highest good and keep your heart and mind open. And take notes.

Dowsing

These final two chapters are devoted to a couple of phenomena that aren't always considered physical mediumship, but which I feel deserve some space and thought—dowsing/pendulum and spoon bending.

In both phenomena, your own mind and body come into play—you tune into your inner self and the wisdom that resides there, rather than connecting with a separate physical entity. There's no ectoplasm making the pendulum move or Spirit entities coming through your body in the form of automatic writing or trance channeling. Yet there's something very interesting going on that, if you connect to it, can help build your trust with Spirit and your higher self and help your conscious mind get past its limiting beliefs.

Dowsing has been practiced for centuries, often to discover natural resources, such as water. When you think of dowsing, you may think of a Y-shaped stick, held with both hands on the forked part. That's one way of dowsing. Today, dowsing is most often practiced using a pendulum.

Pendulums have been used for eons as a way of connecting with Spirit and divining answers to our myriad of questions as we navigate this human experience. They're simple to use and a way to connect with your intuition.

How pendulums work

Divination using a pendulum really isn't all that mysterious. The answers come from within your inner, wiser self (hello, intuition!). It's connected to your ideomotor response, a mind-body connection that causes slight muscular movements independent of your conscious desires or emotions.

Skeptics think of the ideomotor response as an unconscious reaction to a stimulus and use this explanation to disregard tools such a pendulums or phenomena like automatic writing and table tipping. However, I consider it to be a mind-body connection that taps into your intuition to give you signals that can be translated into clearer answers using a pendulum. Intuition uses your body all the time to give you information—a sinking feeling in your stomach, a tug in your gut, the rising of your heart with inspiration or excitement.

A pendulum is just a tool to interpret these body sensations. The trick here is that you need to detach your emotions and expectations from the answers you receive so that you can access your intuition and higher self.

What to use as your pendulum

You can use many different things as pendulums—any slightly weighted object can work. You could use a rock, crystal, pendant or ring, for example. Hang it from a chain, string or ribbon—something that allows it to hang straight and move easily. The chain should be 4-15" long—whatever feels right to you. Many people like to purchase a crystal pendulum with a chain to use specifically for work with Spirit; others are happy using a necklace or putting a special ring on a chain. As long as it hangs straight and moves easily and evenly, it should work.

How to hold and use your pendulum

When you begin working with a pendulum, do so in a quiet, peaceful place. Whether that's the middle of the woods or your living room is up to you. But you should be free from distractions and interruptions.

Hold the chain between your thumb and forefinger with your writing hand, letting the weighted part hang. Relax your hand and fingers.

Before setting up communication with your pendulum—which you'll want to check each time you use it, not just the first time—give yourself a moment to settle yourself and get centered. Take some deep breaths, allow yourself to set aside the cares and worries you usually carry around with you, and connect with Spirit. Ask for your highest and best good and trust that's what you'll receive.

Setting up communication with your pendulum

Before you can ask Spirit questions via your pendulum, you need to learn how your pendulum will communicate with you. There are a few ways to do this which are outlined below.

Tell it what you want yes and no to be

Deliberately move the pendulum in clockwise circles or backwards and forwards and ask it to always indicate a *yes* or a positive response with that movement.

Then deliberately move the pendulum in anti-clockwise circles or side to side and ask it to use that movement to indicate a *no* or a negative response.

Similarly, you can use a printed pendulum chart with responses indicated on it and instruct your pendulum to use that to communicate with you.

Some pendulums are responsive to this. Others appear to have resistance to being told what to do and want to use their own method.

Ask the pendulum

Ask your pendulum to show you *yes* and *no* and wait to see how it swings each time. First, ask for *yes* and wait, allowing the pendulum to swing as it will. Then ask for *no* and wait until you get a response.

You can also ask questions with yes/no answers—questions you already know the answer to, that are solid, objective and grounded in reality. Like: *Is it Wednesday today? Is it daytime? Is my name legal name currently Joanna?* All questions you ask your pendulum need to be specific—for instance, my soul name isn't Joanna, and my legal name hasn't always been Joanna. But it is currently, and my pendulum will answer yes to that.

Another way is to visualize a happy or successful moment in your life or feeling within yourself. I like to imagine my children or partner hugging me and telling me, "I love you." The pendulum will respond to this positive emotion with a *yes* response. Then remember a time of sadness, sorrow or deep disappointment. The pendulum will respond to this different emotion with its movement for *no*.

For some people, when the pendulum swings left to right (like the shaking of your head), it means *no*. When it swings backward and forward (like nodding your head) it means *yes*. Swinging in a circular movement means uncertainty: *maybe, not now, ask again later*. But the pattern might be different for you. A clockwise motion may mean *yes*, while counterclockwise may mean *no*. That's why you start with some objective questions to determine how your pendulum will give answers and information.

Trust your intuition here. There are times I've asked a question and have received a weak response from the pendulum and have heard within myself that I didn't phrase the question specifically enough or that it's information I don't need to know right now.

Using your pendulum

Now that you've got your pendulum set up with whichever method that works for you, you can begin using it.

There's probably no limit to what you can use a pendulum for—basically anything you can ask questions about. Here are some of the major areas that people use often pendulums for.

Finding something that's lost

Pendulums can be very helpful in finding lost items, people and pets. How you use it depends on how narrow or wide the scope of where you're looking is.

In a room

Ask the pendulum where the object is located. The pendulum will swing in its direction. Move in that direction and notice if and how the pendulum changes. Keep going until you find the item.

You can also do this in conjunction with clairsentience, feeling where the object is as a tug in your gut, or tapping into your clairvoyant abilities and seeing where the item is. Often, as you ask the pendulum to lead you to the object, you'll receive information about it through your intuitive senses as well.

Physical mediumship – Pendulum dowsing

In a house

Go through your house, room by room or in your mind, and ask the pendulum, *is the object is in this room?* You'll receive a *yes* or *no* response for each room.

Once you've narrowed it down to a specific room, go into that room and ask where the object is located.

On a map

You'll need a map for this. It doesn't matter, as far as I can tell, if it's a paper map you can fold out flat or a map you pull up on your smartphone or tablet. But you want to be able to hold the pendulum over it.

Ask the pendulum if the object is in the area of the map. You'll get a yes or no answer. If yes, point to places on the map, or zoom into it if it's on a digital display, to narrow down the location. You may also feel the pendulum tug or pull toward a specific location, which is why it's helpful to have it on a flat surface.

If you're looking for a person or pet, it can be helpful to have a photo or object of belonging to the person to tune into their energy frequency.

Making decisions

A pendulum can be used to find answers to anything you can ask a yes/no question about. *Will I live until I'm 120? Should I move to Hawaii? Does my cat have cancer?*

Prepare your question in advance, either in your mind or by writing it down. Get clear and calm within yourself (meditation is great for this), then ask your question. Allow your mind to relax and empty and wait for the pendulum's response.

It turns out that there are a whole lot of things about this life I don't want to know the answers to ahead of time. Do you really want to know when you're going to die? Or if your kids will grow up healthy and give you grandkids? Or if your latest book will be a best seller? I think there are some things we're supposed to find out as we go along—not try and skip ahead in the book of our lives to find out how it all works out. But you have free will and may feel differently.

Choosing between several options

You can also use your pendulum to get information from Spirit if there are several things you're trying to choose between—such as houses you're looking at purchasing, supplements you're thinking of taking, people you're thinking of marrying, anything that has more than 1 or 2 choices.

Set out the various options, or representations of them, such as a photo, on a flat surface. Hold your pendulum over each option, moving very slowly. Wait to feel a downwards tug or pull over one of the options. The pendulum may also feel very heavy before it tugs. Keep going over all the options until you've moved over all of them—you may feel a tug on more than one, so you want to discern which has the strongest pull.

Connecting with Spirit

Your pendulum can also be used as a tool to activate your mental mediumship abilities.

By holding a pendulum over an object, you may be able to tune into it with psychometry and begin to receive stronger impressions with your intuitive senses, perhaps seeing, hearing, or feeling information about the object and its former owner(s).

You can also use a pendulum to connect with Spirit entities in a place, especially if you feel like there's a Spirit presence around. You can use the pendulum in its many ways—to locate where the Spirit is in a room, building or area, to ask questions of the Spirit, and as a magnifier of your intuitive senses to get clearer information about it.

Using a pendulum in this way does several things. First, it helps you connect in with your inner self, allowing you to access your intuitive self, which is what you need to open and use your clairsenses. Second, it's a tool, which can give you confidence. It seems easier for many people to trust a tool, whether that's a pendulum, a tarot card deck or anything external to them, than it is to simply trust themselves and the information they get. Lastly, the crystal structure of the pendulum itself can help to focus and magnify energy. When I do phone sessions with clients, I'll often hold a quartz rod to amplify the energy and make a more solid connection to my client and their loved ones in Spirit. I don't technically need it but, especially if the energy feels low for some reason, it definitely helps. Plus, gems are pretty and feel good.

Things to keep in mind

If you're not getting satisfying results using your pendulum, here are some things to keep in mind as you work with it.

Maintain emotional detachment from the outcome

If you're getting confusing or contradicting answers, take an emotional step back. The pendulum allows you to make full use of your combined conscious and unconscious knowledge. But you need to disconnect from what you think you want. Ask for your highest good and let go of the answer itself.

The best frame of mind to be in is one of childlike innocence, expectancy and wonder.

This can be understandably hard, as you wouldn't be asking questions if you didn't care about the answer. But it's vital to let go of expectations and do what you need to get into a quiet, centered place before doing pendulum work.

Ask specific questions

Sometimes the answers still don't come clearly. If so, ask clarifying questions. You may not be phrasing your question clearly.

I've found that you need to ask specific questions that can't be interpreted in multiple ways. Those get the strongest, clearest responses.

Accept you may not be supposed to know

There are things you're not supposed to know right now.

Your intuition works right here in the present. It shines the light of Spirit on the very next steps on your path—because those are the only steps you can actually take. You can't walk on your path of a year from now, only on your path today. So perhaps knowing if you'll be in a different job or house or with a different partner one, five or 10 years from now isn't something you truly need to know (although it may be something you want to know).

Trust that, if you've asked for your highest good, that's what you're receiving.

Spoon bending

Spoon bending is a form of psychokinesis—the ability to manipulate matter using your mind. Many forms of physical mediumship fall under the label of psychokinesis as, while the information isn't coming through your mind, you do use your mind to control your body to produce physical mediumship phenomena.

I'm not sure if spoon bending is truly physical mediumship, but I'm including it here because it's an excellent way to learn to let go of limiting beliefs. Once you've felt a solid metal spoon get soft and easily bend through the power of your thought and intention, it tends to open you mind to new possibilities. If you can do that, what else can you do?

The basics of spoon bending are this: you concentrate your energy on a metal spoon and, when it suddenly feels soft and pliable, you bend and twist the spoon with little resistance until it begins to get difficult to move again easily. In theory, you can make the spoon bend without using any physical force at all. But even using your hands, you can feel a clear difference in the strength of the spoon and its ability to easily bend.

It requires a willingness to let go of your belief that spoons are solid, non-bending objects (or that they require a great deal of physical force to bend), and the ability to feel the energy of the spoon so that you know when to bend it.

How to practice spoon bending

There are several methods you can use to bend spoons. The most important thing is to get out of your own way and allow it to happen.

Physical mediumship – Spoon bending

First, get a spoon you don't mind bending. I like to get spoons and forks from thrift stores for spoon bending. Choose a spoon that's not so thin and weak you can easily bend it with just muscle strength, but not so incredibly thick that you need tools to bend it.

This latter isn't because it's a physical trick, but rather so that your mind believes it might be possible to do.

Find a comfortable spot where you won't be disturbed. Take a deep breath in. Then let it out. Know that only your highest and best good will come to you. Set your intention: "I will bend this spoon."

Hold the spoon in both your hands. Flex it a little and feel the natural resistance of the metal. Then do any of the following exercises until the spoon is ready to bend.

You'll know your spoon is ready to bend when it feels pliable. The metal will soften and become like taffy. Ever seen hard candy being made? When it's at a certain temperature, it's soft and pliable, able to be stretched. But when it cools, it sets, becoming hard. The spoon will feel like that. It'll get soft for a moment or two, maybe a few seconds, then it'll firm up again.

Counting (and breathing)

Decide that, when you get to 10, the spoon is going to bend for you.

Inhale 1. Exhale 2.

Inhale 3. Exhale 4.

Inhale 5. Exhale 6.

Inhale 7. Exhale 8.

Inhale 9. Exhale 10, applying a little pressure to the spoon. It's ready to bend when it feels pliable and soft.

If it doesn't want to give, that's OK. Keep breathing. If it does bend, keep bending and twisting it for as long as it feels soft. Then stop and take a look.

Getting excited

Some people like to command the spoon to bend. As you hold the spoon and breathe, slowly and deeply, say, "Bend, spoon, bend!" You can repeat this several times until the spoon becomes pliable.

You can also try jumping up and down to raise your energy. Or even shouting. (I don't like shouting at spoons myself, but I hear it works for some folks.)

Singing to the spoon

Do you know the tune, "Sun, sun, Mr. golden sun, please shine down on me?" Sometimes I like to sing to my spoon: "Spoon, spoon, Mr. bendy spoon, please will you bend for me?"

It sounds ridiculous, but it works. The combination of song and the silliness of it raises my vibration—and that of the spoon—and distracts me enough to allow the spoon to bend.

Realize that everything is energy

My most successful way of bending spoons is knowing that everything in this world is made up of energy. It just vibrates at different frequencies. The spoon is more solid than I am. But it doesn't have to be. People in Spirit are less solid than I am, but I raise the frequency of my vibration and use my intuitive senses to be able to sense them and communicate with them.

Hold the spoon in both hands. Become aware of the energy of your own body. Feel the energy of your aura, right around your body.

Extend your energy to the spoon. Allow the spoon to become infused with your energy.

Know that we are all one, from the same source energy, all connected.

Know that just as you can bend the fingers of your hand, so too can you bend the spoon. Imagine it as part of your body, part of your hand.

Then bend it.

You can also imagine the distance between the protons and electrons in the spoon's atoms increasing. This makes it pliable and easy to bend.

The benefits of spoon bending

Beyond creating cutlery that's no longer good for its original intended use, spoon bending does a few things for me:

- It helps me focus my energy. I can only bend spoons when I'm in a quiet, focused frame of mind.
- It reminds me that we're all energy and that all energy is connected.
- I feel connected to Spirit.
- It makes me ponder what else is possible. When I'm having a hard moment or something feels too difficult to surmount, I look at my twisted-up cutlery and think, "Huh, well, that wasn't impossible. I did that. I can do this too."

Physical mediumship – Spoon bending

I took my kids to a spoon-bending workshop once (because they'll learn things from other people so much better than they'll learn them from their own mother), and they had a great experience. This is what my son, who was 10 at the time, said about it.

> *"At first, it was difficult and frustrating because I couldn't do it. But then as soon as I did it once, it felt like I could do it another time and another time and another time and it was really fun."*

> *"It felt like a hard object at first before I bent the spoon. Then as I bent the spoon it felt 20 times weaker and then it just went flop and I could bend it. I felt very accomplished."*

Consider how you might feel on your journey once you know that seemingly impossible things are actually quite possible. Give yourself the freedom to move forward on your path, trusting in Spirit and in yourself.

Conclusion

If you've given these exercises a try with your mediumship development circle, you've given yourself and your circle members opportunities to develop your abilities in all sorts of ways.

As I said in the introduction to this book, a mediumship development circle is a place to learn and grow. It's a place to make connections with yourself and develop a friendly relationship with the deeper parts of you. It's a place to connect with Spirit and the world beyond what you usually experience in your everyday reality. And it's a place to connect with others of like mind and like heart.

I remain friends with several people from my first development circles and even those folks I don't see or talk to regularly hold a special place in my heart and memories.

Pretty much everything you want to develop an ability for requires you to put in time and effort. You learn to write better by spending time writing. You learn to develop mediumship abilities by spending time sitting with Spirit and practicing. That means taking in information from Spirit in a safe and controlled way and also giving out the information you get. This develops the trust needed to truly believe in the work you're doing.

So what comes next?

What do you want to come next? Many mediums don't become professional mediums, hanging up their shingle and doing readings for the public. I want you to know that it's perfectly OK to not charge money for your gift and to use it solely to serve your circle, church and friends and family. It's also OK to offer your mediumship on a professional level and either supplement your income with it or have it be your sole living.

I've done both and they both have their merits. As I'm writing this book, I no longer offer mediumship readings to the public, although I still serve my home church and connect to my own loved ones in Spirit. I don't know what the future holds, but I'm open to it.

There's a lot to consider when deciding what your next steps are. First ask your own inner wisdom. Is this the right next step for you?

Then consider your personality and interpersonal skills. Are you ready to counsel the bereaved and skeptical when they come to you for healing? Because that's what mediumship is ultimately here for. It's a means of bridging the divide between the life we experience now and the one we'll have once our physical bodies no longer house us. That divide can cause so much pain due to the unfinished business, things left unsaid, things we wish we, or the other person, hadn't said or done. Your role as a medium is to be that conduit.

I took what felt like a long break from mediumship between 2009 and 2014 while moving across the country with young kids, getting divorced, working full time and getting remarried and acquiring two more kids in the process. When I began offering readings professionally in 2014, I wasn't quite sure if I still had it. I did. Running my own home development circle undoubtedly helped immensely, as it gave me time to sit with Spirit, replenish myself and connect with others.

I wish you the best on your journey, wherever it leads you.

References and further reading

These are some of the books that helped guide me in my own development and in the writing of this book.

- A Guide to Mediumship by M.H. and E.W. Wallis
- The Art of Mediumship by Elaine Kuzmeskus
- Finding the Spirit Within by Linda Williamson
- The Home Circle, Booklet 2 in the Sunflower Series by Marilyn Awtry
- The Idiot's Guide to Communicating with Spirits by Rita S. Berkowitz and Deborah S. Romain
- Medium: A Step-by-Step Guide to Communicating with the Spirit World by Konstanza Morning Star
- Mediumship Mastery: The Mechanics of Receiving Spirit Communications by Stephen A. Hermann
- Psychic Abilities for Beginners: Awaken Your Intuitive Senses by Melanie Barnum

Thanks and acknowledgements

I have so many people to thank for helping me move forward on my journey of teaching mediumship.

First, there's everyone I've sat in a home development circle with. I have such fond memories of our circles, the camaraderie we shared and our growth together. Those remain some of my favorite meditations. Many thanks to John, Regina, Dean, Lisa, Carol, Robyn, Kass, Robin, Tom, Terry, Mary, Cheryl and more for sharing that time with me.

I'm grateful to my students for trusting me to guide them in their development and letting me experiment on them with new exercises I came up with, including Kelsang, Theresa, Jill, Angel, Rich, Leah, Laura, Alice and more. Extra special thanks for Jill for being one of my first readers and to Kelsang for always encouraging me and providing me with a template for a mediumship development circle agreement. I've never been quite that thorough.

I owe a huge thanks to Connie Wake and Sue Fiandach. You both pushed me to do this work. I remember moaning to you about how there were no circles where I lived. Connie looked at me and said, "Well, start one yourself." When I felt blank and overwhelmed at the idea of running my own circle, Sue gave me ideas for exercises, some of which are in this book.

Thank you to Phoebe and her online development circle for trying out some of these zany exercises and giving me helpful confirmation and feedback.

Thanks and acknowledgements

I'm also grateful to my medium colleagues, who are also out there teaching others. This is an incomplete list, but it includes Travis Sanders, Melanie Barnum, Konstanza Morningstar and Stephen Hermann. Your books and work have been inspiring to me and I'm glad the next generation of mediums is in your capable hands and hearts.

Thanks also to various local cafes for letting me work on this book away from the distraction of my home while providing a little caffeine including Sundial Café, Allan Bros and Market of Choice.

Lastly, thanks to my lovely family who continue to love and support me, no matter where my Spirit-led life takes me, and to Spirit for shining the light of my highest good on my path.

About the author

I'm not a fan of talking about myself in the third person.

I'm an ordained Spiritualist minister and certified medium with the National Spiritualist Association of Churches. Originally from England, I live in the lovely West Coast town of Eugene, Oregon, with my wonderful (third) husband and our blended family of four children (one may have moved out by the time this book is published).

I teach the sensitives, helpers and healers of the world to heal from loss and learn to trust themselves and their inner voice again. Developing intuition and mediumship abilities can be part of this process.

I've taught classes in spiritual development—including mediumship and intuition—to many dozens of students since 2001 and have helped hundreds of clients find healing and meaning in their losses, through grief counseling and mediumship work. Through expressing myself in writing, I became an award-winning journalist and the author of eight published books.

As an independently-published author, it'd mean a whole lot to me if you'd review this book on your favorite online bookstore so that other people can know what to expect and whether they should read it themselves.

Stay in touch

You're welcome to keep in touch with me in whatever way works best for you.

Learn more about me and my work at www.revjoannabartlettlight.com where you can subscribe to my newsletter and get regular updates from me with my latest tips, tools and teachings.

You can also connect with me on:

YouTube: www.youtube.com/c/RevJoannaBartlett

Facebook: www.facebook.com/revjoannabartlett

Instagram: www.instagram.com/revjoannabartlett

www.ingramcontent.com/pod-product-compliance
Lightning Source LLC
Chambersburg PA
CBHW030111100526
44591CB00009B/361